Angels
a Knitter's dozen

by Gerdine Strong

Angels
a Knitter's dozen

by Gerdine Strong

Angels: A Knitter's Dozen
PUBLISHED BY XRX BOOKS

PUBLISHER
Alexis Yiorgos Xenakis

EDITOR
Elaine Rowley

EDITORIAL ASSISTANT
Sue Nelson

KNITTING EDITOR
Joni Coniglio

GRAPHIC DESIGNER
Bob Natz

PHOTOGRAPHER
Alexis Yiorgos Xenakis

DIRECTOR, PUBLISHING SERVICES
David Xenakis

PRODUCTION DIRECTOR
Dennis Pearson

BOOK PRODUCTION MANAGER
Natalie Sorenson

DIGITAL COLOR SPECIALIST
Jason Bittner

PRODUCTION
Everett Baker

TECHNICAL ILLUSTRATIONS
Jay Reeve
Carol Skallerud

FIRST PUBLISHED IN USA IN 2002 BY XRX, INC.

ISBN 1-893762-12-2

Produced by XRX, Inc.,
PO Box 1525,
Sioux Falls, SD 57101-1525 605.338.2450

Contents

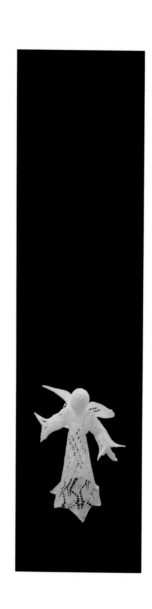

Made of 7 simple pieces, these angels are a great introduction to lace knitting and make wonderful projects for intermediate knitters.

But . . . I don't knit lace.
Small pieces and simple lace patterns, worked one at a time, make this a good place to start. *Lace Basics,* on page 48, is especially for you.

But . . . I don't know how to use double-pointed needles.
Turn to *School for Angels*, page 50. Five of the pieces for each angel are worked back and forth using 2 double-pointed needles as straight needles.

But . . . I've never used fine cotton and fine needles.
Practice with a swatch of garter stitch or stockinette, and turn to page 49.

But . . . I don't know how to shape, stiffen, and put the pieces together.
See our step-by-step, illustrated instructions on page 46.

But . . . I know all that.
Then sit back, knit, and enjoy this interesting and unique series. The similarities bring comfort; the differences add interest.

But . . . I want to give an angel to a friend who golfs.
Craft shops offer a large selection of props that will fit the angels. Some doll house accessories are the right size. This means that angels could march down the dining room table carrying in Christmas dinner—turkey, peas and carrots, mashed potatoes, cranberry sauce, mince tarts, and plum pudding (a raisin on a bottle cap liner). Plastic golf clubs, tennis rackets, and baseball bats and balls can be painted with gold or silver model paint. Save crystal miniatures for special-occasion angels.

The first two of my angels are knitters—one knits her second wing and the other knits a gold wing for the higher-ups. The angels stand well on their own or hang as ornaments. The easiest order for knitting is: arms, wings, bodice, skirt, and head. This means the knitter can see the lace pattern develop before the skirt is knit.

2nd-wing-knitting Angel

SIZE
3½" high

YARN
Coats & Clark • Knit-Cro-Sheen
100% cotton
225yds/205m
1 ball

NEEDLES
2.25mm/US1 double-pointed
needles (dpn) Set of 5

EXTRAS
Cornstarch
Tapestry needle
Polyester fiberfill or cotton ball
Gold-painted wooden
cocktail picks for knitting needles

Notes 1 See *School,* page 50 for lifted increase, ssk, SK2P and S2KP2. **2** Arms, Wings, and Bodice are worked back and forth with 2 dpn; Head and Skirt are worked circularly. **3** In Canada: Use Coats & Clark's "Mercerized" (1,000m ball). **4** Charts are on pages 6–7.

2nd-WING-KNITTING ANGEL

Arms *MAKE 2*
Cast on 7 sts. Work 20 rows of Arms Chart. Fasten off last st.

Complete wing *MAKE 1*
Cast on 7 sts. Work 24 rows of 2nd-wing-knitting Angel Wing Chart. Fasten off last st.

Partial wing *MAKE 1*
Work as for complete wing, ending in center of row 11. Place sts on hold. Cut yarn, leaving a 1-yard tail. Wind this yarn into a miniature ball and let hang.

Bodice
Cast on 7 sts. Work 26 rows of 2nd-wing-knitting Angel Bodice Chart. Bind off remaining 5 sts.

Skirt
With crochet hook, chain 16, join with slip st to form ring. *With hook, pick up a st in each chain st and transfer sts evenly to 4 dpn.

Rnd 1 Work 4-st repeat of 2nd-wing-knitting Angel Skirt Chart 4 times. Continue in chart pattern through rnd 21—48 sts. **Rnd 22** K1, *yo, k9, yo, twist left-hand needle with remaining 2 sts counterclockwise to become right-hand needle (equivalent of sl2tog), then k1 from next needle, p2sso; repeat from*. Pass last sl2tog over k1 from first needle—48 sts. **23, 25** Knit. **24** *Yo, ssk; repeat from*. With crochet hook, work single-crochet bind-off (see page 6).

Head
Cast on 9 sts and divide evenly onto 3 dpn. **Rnds 1 and 3** Knit. **2** *K1, lifted increase into 2nd st, k1; repeat from*—12 sts. **4** *K1, lifted increase into 2nd st; repeat from*—18 sts. **5–8** Knit. **9** *K1, ssk; repeat from*—12 sts. **10 and 12** Knit. **11** *K1, ssk, k1; repeat from*—9 sts. Cut yarn and pull through remaining loops. Do not pull tightly.

Finishing
Follow instructions for Gold-wing-knitting Angel on page 4.

3

I developed the original angel in 1988 for the Festival of Trees, a fund-raising event for the Children's Hospital Research Foundation. While sewing plastic musical instruments to the first angels, I thought, when I get to heaven, I don't want to play a musical instrument—I want to knit!

2 Gold-wing-knitting Angel

SIZE
3½" high

YARN
Coats & Clark • Knit-Cro-Sheen
100% cotton
225yds/205m
1 ball

NEEDLES
2.25mm/US1 double-pointed
needles (dpn) Set of 5

EXTRAS
Crochet hook of comparable size
Cornstarch
Tapestry needle
Polyester fiberfill or cotton ball
Gold-painted wooden
cocktail picks for knitting needles
Small amount of
gold metallic yarn

Notes 1 See *School,* page 50 for lifted increase, ssk, SK2P and S2KP2. **2** Arms, Wings, and Bodice are worked back and forth with 2 dpn; Head and Skirt are worked circularly. **3** In Canada: Use Coats & Clark's "Mercerized" (1,000m ball). **4** Charts are on pages 6-7.

GOLD-WING-KNITTING ANGEL

Arms *MAKE 2*

Cast on 7 sts. Work 20 rows of Arms Chart. Fasten off last st.

Complete wings *MAKE 2*

Cast on 5 sts. Work 22 rows of Gold-wing-knitting Angel Wing Chart. Fasten off last st.

Partial wing *MAKE 1*

With gold metallic yarn, work as for complete wing, ending in center of row 11. Place sts on hold. Cut yarn, leaving a 1-yard tail. Wind this yarn into a miniature ball and let hang.

Bodice

Cast on 7 sts. Work 25 rows of Gold-wing-knitting Angel Bodice Chart. Bind off remaining 7 sts.

Skirt

With crochet hook, chain 16, join with slip st to form ring. *With hook, pick up a st in each chain st and transfer sts evenly to 4 dpn.

Rnd 1 Work 4-st repeat of Gold-wing-knitting Angel Skirt Chart 4 times. Continue in chart pattern through rnd 25—56 sts. With crochet hook, work single-crochet bind-off (see page 6).

Head

Cast on 9 sts and divide evenly onto 3 dpn. **Rnds 1 and 3** Knit. **2** *K1, lifted increase into 2nd st, k1; repeat from*—12 sts. **4** *K1, lifted increase into 2nd st; repeat from*—18 sts. **5–8** Knit. **9** *K1, ssk; repeat from*—12 sts. **10 and 12** Knit. **11** *K1, ssk, k1; repeat from*—9 sts. Cut yarn and pull through remaining loops. Do not pull tightly.

Finishing

Darn in ends at lower edge of skirt and tips of wings before stiffening. Use other ends for joining pieces and to hold accessories. See *How to Assemble an Angel,* page 46.

Add knitting Place open sts of partial wings on cocktail sticks. Use yarn at end of hands to hold knitting needles.

5

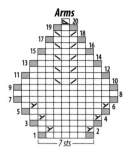

Arms

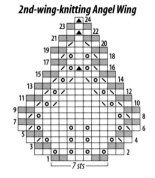

2nd-wing-knitting Angel Wing

Single-crochet Bind-Off

Insert hook knitwise into first knit st. Yarn round hook, pull up a loop and drop knit st. *Insert hook in next st, yarn round hook, pull up a loop and drop knit st—2 loops on hook. Yarn round hook and pull up a loop through both sts on hook— 1 single-crochet bind-off complete. Repeat from*. Cut yarn.

For a continuous, smooth edge, go through first bound-off st, then down through the last bound-off st again (see below). Weave in end.

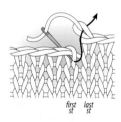

first st *last st*

in other words…

ARMS CHART
BEGIN ON 7 STS

Row 1 and all WS rows K1, p to last st, k1. **2, 4 and 6** K into front and back of st, k to last 2 sts, k into front and back of st, k1. **8** Knit—13 sts. **10** K4, k2tog, k1, ssk, k4. **12** K3, k2tog, k1, ssk, k3. **14** K2, k2tog, k1, ssk, k2. **16** K1, k2tog, k1, ssk, k1. **18** K2tog, k1, ssk—3 sts. **20** SK2P.

2ND-WING-KNITTING ANGEL WING CHART
BEGIN ON 7 STS

Row 1 and all WS rows (except 23) K2, p to last 2 sts, k2. **2** K2, [yo, k1] 4 times, k1. **4** K1, ssk, yo, k2, yo, k1, yo, k2, yo, k2tog, k1. **6** K1, ssk, yo, k3, yo, k1, yo, k3, yo, k2tog, k1—15 sts. **8** K1, ssk, yo, k9, yo, k2tog, k1. **10** K1, ssk, yo, ssk, k5, k2tog, yo, k2tog, k1. **12** K1, ssk, yo, ssk, k3, k2tog, yo, k2tog, k1. **14** K1, ssk, yo, ssk, k1, k2tog, yo, k2tog, k1. **16** K1, ssk, yo, S2KP2, yo, k2tog, k1. **18** K1, ssk, yo, k1, yo, k2tog, k1. **20** K1, ssk, k1, k2tog, k1. **22** K1, S2KP2, k1. **23** K1, p1, k1. **24** S2KP2.

2ND-WING-KNITTING ANGEL BODICE CHART
BEGIN ON 7 STS

Row 1 and all WS rows K2, p to last 2 sts, k2. **2** K2, [yo, k1] 4 times, k1. **4** K1, ssk, yo, k2, yo, k1, yo, k2, yo, k2tog, k1. **6** K1, ssk, yo, k3, yo, k1, yo, k3, yo, k2tog, k1—15 sts. **8, 10, 12, 14, 16, 18** K1, ssk, yo, k9, yo, k2tog, k1. **20, 22, 24** K1, ssk, yo, ssk, k to last 5 sts, k2tog, yo, k2tog, k1. **26** K1, ssk, S2KP2, k2tog, k1.

2ND-WING-KNITTING ANGEL SKIRT CHART
4 TO 14 TO 12-ST REPEAT

Rnd 1 and all odd-numbered rnds Knit. **2** *[K1, yo] twice, k2; rep from*—24 sts. **4** *K2, yo, k1, yo, k3; rep from*—32 sts. **6** *K3, yo, k1, yo, k4; rep from*—40 sts. **8** *Yo, ssk, k5, k2tog, yo, k1; rep from*. **10** *Yo, k1, yo, ssk, k3, k2tog, yo, k1, yo, k1; rep from*—48 sts. **12** *Yo, k3, yo, ssk, k1, k2tog, yo, k3, yo, k1; rep from*—56 sts. **14** *K3, k2tog, yo, S2KP2, yo, ssk, k4; rep from*—48 sts. **16** *K2, k2tog, yo, k3, yo, ssk, k3; rep from*. **18** *K1, k2tog, yo, k5, yo, ssk, k2; rep from*. **20** *K2tog, yo, k7, yo, ssk, k1; rep from*. **21** Knit.

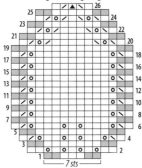

2nd-wing-knitting Angel Bodice

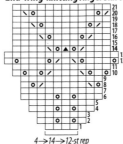

2nd-wing-knitting Angel Skirt

4→14→12-st rep

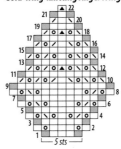

Gold-wing-knitting Angel Wing

5 sts

GOLD-WING-KNITTING ANGEL WING CHART
BEGIN ON 5 STS

Row 1 and all WS rows K1, p to last st, k1.
2 K1, yo, k3, yo, k1. **4** K1, yo, k2tog, yo, k1, yo, ssk, yo, k1. **6** K1, yo, k2tog, yo, k3, yo, ssk, yo, k1. **8** K1, yo, k2tog, yo, k5, yo, ssk, yo, k1—13 sts. **10** [Ssk, yo] twice, ssk, k1, k2tog, [yo, k2tog] twice. **12** [Ssk, yo] twice, S2KP2, [yo, k2tog] twice. **14** [Ssk, yo] twice, k1, [yo, k2tog] twice. **16** Ssk, yo, ssk, k1, k2tog, yo, k2tog. **18** Ssk, yo, S2KP2, yo, k2tog. **20** Ssk, k1, k2tog. **22** S2KP2.

GOLD-WING-KNITTING ANGEL BODICE CHART
BEGIN ON 7 STS

Row 1 and all WS rows K1, p to last st, k1. **2, 4 and 6** K1, yo, k2tog, yo, k to last 3 sts, yo, ssk, yo, k1. **8, 10, 12, 14, 16, 18** [Ssk, yo] twice, k5, [yo, k2tog] twice. **20** [Ssk, yo] twice, ssk, k1, k2tog, [yo, k2tog] twice. **22** [Ssk, yo] twice, S2KP2, [yo, k2tog] twice. **24** Ssk, yo, ssk, k1, k2tog, yo, k2tog. **25** K1, p5, k1.

GOLD-WING-KNITTING ANGEL SKIRT CHART
4 TO 14-ST REPEAT

Rnd 1 and all odd-numbered rnds Knit.
2 *K1, yo, k3, yo; rep from*—24 sts. **4** *K1, yo, k2tog, yo, k1, yo, ssk, yo; rep from*—32 sts. **6** *K1, yo, k2tog, yo, k3, yo, ssk, yo; rep from*—40 sts. **8** *K1, yo, k2tog, yo, k5, yo, ssk, yo; rep from*—48 sts. **10** *K1, yo, k2tog, yo, k7, yo, ssk, yo; rep from*—56 sts. **12** *K2, [yo, ssk] twice, k3, [k2tog, yo] twice, k1; rep from*. **14** *K3, [yo, ssk] twice, k1, [k2tog, yo] twice, k2; rep from*. **16** *K4, yo, ssk, yo, S2KP2, yo, k2tog, yo, k3; rep from*. **18** *K5, yo, ssk, k1, k2tog, yo, k4; rep from*. **20** *K6, yo, S2KP2, yo, k5; rep from*. **22** *K5, k2tog, yo, k1, yo, ssk, k4; rep from*. **24** *Yo, ssk; rep from*. **25** Knit.

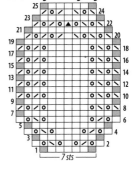

Gold-wing-knitting Angel Bodice

7 sts

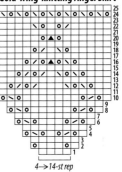

Gold-wing-knitting Angel Skirt

4→14-st rep

Both these angels' skirts are knitted from the top to the bottom. If you only have a set of 4 double-pointed needles, then place 2 repeats on one needle and one on each of the other two. This makes it easier to see the logic of the lace pattern, and each needle begins a repeat.

Ball-winding Angel

SIZE
3½" high

YARN
Coats & Clark • Knit-Cro-Sheen
100% cotton
225yds/205m
1 ball

NEEDLES
2.25mm/US1
double-pointed needles (dpn)
Set of 5

EXTRAS
Crochet hook of comparable size
Cornstarch
Tapestry needle
Polyester fiberfill or cotton ball
White clear-drying glue
2 yds gold metallic yarn
6" of invisible sewing thread

Notes 1 See *School*, p. 50 for ssk, ssp, lifted increase, SK2P, S2KP2, and single-crochet bind-off. **2** Arms, Wings, and Bodice are worked back and forth with 2 dpn. Head and Skirt are worked circularly. **3** In Canada: Use Coats & Clark's "Mercerized" (1,000m ball). **4** Photos on pages 10—11; charts are on pages 12-13.

BALL-WINDING ANGEL
Arms *MAKE 2*
Cast on 7 sts. Work 20 rows of Arms Chart. Fasten off last st.
Right Wing
Cast on 5 sts. Work 21 rows of Ball-winding Angel Right Wing Chart. Fasten off last st.
Left Wing
Cast on 5 sts. Work 21 rows of Ball-winding Angel Left Wing Chart. Fasten off last st.
Bodice
Cast on 7 sts. Work 23 rows of Ball-winding Angel Bodice Chart. Bind off remaining 8 sts.
Skirt
Cast on 16 sts and divide evenly onto 4 dpn. **Rnd 1** Work 4-st repeat of Ball-winding Angel Skirt Chart 4 times. Continue in chart pattern through rnd 25—48 sts. With crochet hook, work single-crochet bind-off.
Head
Cast on 9 sts and divide evenly onto 3 dpn. **Rnds 1 and 3** Knit. **2** *K1, lifted increase into 2nd st, k1; repeat from*—12 sts. **4** *K1, lifted increase into 2nd st; repeat from*—18 sts. **5–8** Knit. **9** *K1, ssk; repeat from*—12 sts. **10 and 12** Knit. **11** *K1, ssk, k1; repeat from*—9 sts. Cut yarn and pull through remaining loops. Do not pull tightly.
Finishing
See Both Angels on next page for finishing.

Skein-holding Angel 4

Notes See Notes for Ball-winding Angel, previous page.

SKEIN-HOLDING ANGEL

Arms MAKE 2
Cast on 7 sts. Work 20 rows of Arms Chart. Fasten off last st.

Right Wing
Cast on 5 sts. Work 22 rows of Skein-holding Angel Right Wing Chart. Fasten off last st.

Left Wing
Cast on 5 sts. Work 22 rows of Skein-holding Angel Left Wing Chart. Fasten off last st.

Bodice
Cast on 7 sts. Work 23 rows of Skein-holding Angel Bodice Chart. Bind off remaining 7 sts.

Skirt
Cast on 16 sts and divide evenly onto 4 dpn. *Rnd 1* Work 4-st repeat of Skein-holding Angel Skirt Chart 4 times. Continue in chart pattern through rnd 25—48 sts. With crochet hook, work single-crochet bind-off.

Head
Cast on 9 sts and divide evenly onto 3 dpn. *Rnds 1 and 3* Knit. *2* *K1, lifted increase into 2nd st, k1; repeat from*—12 sts. *4* *K1, lifted increase into 2nd st; repeat from*—18 sts. *5–8* Knit. *9* *K1, ssk; repeat from*—12 sts. *10 and 12* Knit. *11* *K1, ssk, k1; repeat from*—9 sts. Cut yarn and pull through remaining loops. Do not pull tightly.

Finishing
See Both Angels for Finishing.

Stiffener note
When stiffening arms of Skein-holding Angel, bend the arms at right angles and turn the 'hands' up.

BOTH ANGELS
Darn in ends at lower edge of skirt and tips of wings before stiffening. Use other ends for joining pieces and to hold metallic yarn. See *How to Assemble an Angel*, page 46.

Add ball and skein Wind metallic yarn around 2 or 3 fingers 6-10 times, depending on yarn thickness, for 'skein'. Cut end about 1 yd long. Half hitch skein to hold it; wind ball from cut end, begin with a knot. Leaving 2" between skein and ball, half hitch last 2 winds around ball, and secure using clear-drying glue. Loop yarn at end of hands over skein and darn back into arms. Tether angels together at hem, using invisible sewing thread.

SIZE
3½" high

YARN
Coats & Clark · Knit-Cro-Sheen
100% cotton
225yds/205m
1 ball

NEEDLES
2.25mm/US1
double-pointed needles (dpn)
Set of 5

EXTRAS
Crochet hook of comparable size
Cornstarch
Tapestry needle
Polyester fiberfill or cotton ball
White clear-drying glue
2 yds gold metallic yarn
6" of invisible sewing thread

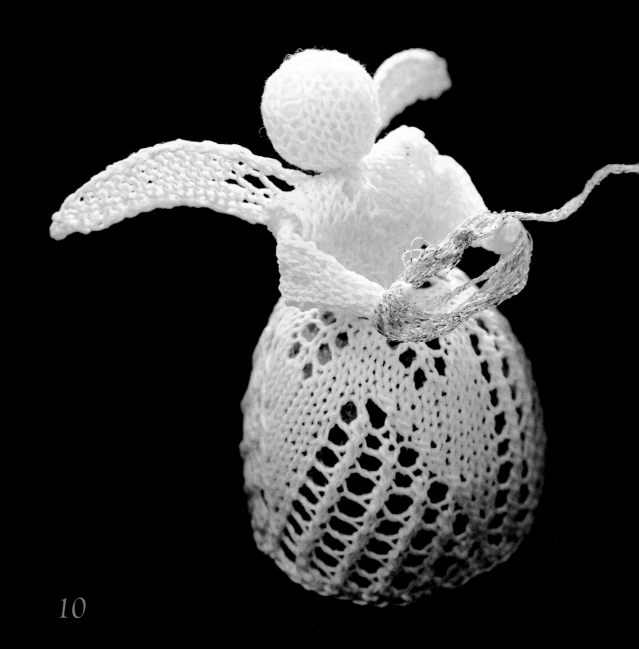

10

11

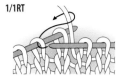

1/1RT

1 Knit second stitch on left-hand needle, working in front of first stitch,…

2 …then knit first stitch,…

3 … slip both stitches off needle.

1/1LT

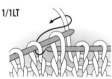

1 With right-hand needle behind left-hand needle, knit second stitch on left-hand needle,…

2 …then knit first stitch,…

3 …slip both stitches off needle.

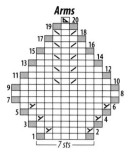

Arms

7 sts

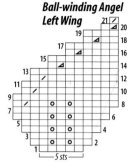

Ball-winding Angel Left Wing

5 sts

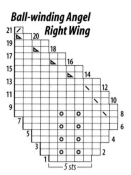

Ball-winding Angel Right Wing

5 sts

in other words…

ARMS CHART
BEGIN ON 7 STS

Row 1 and all WS rows K1, p to last st, k1. *2, 4 and 6* K into front and back of st, k to last 2 sts, k into front and back of st, k1. *8* Knit—13 sts. *10* K4, k2tog, k1, ssk, k4. *12* K3, k2tog, k1, ssk, k3. *14* K2, k2tog, k1, ssk, k2. *16* K1, k2tog, k1, ssk, k1. *18* K2tog, k1, ssk—3 sts. *20* SK2P.

BALL-WINDING ANGEL RIGHT WING CHART
BEGIN ON 5 STS

Row 1 and all WS rows (except 21) Purl. *2* K2, yo, k1, yo, k2—7 sts. *4* K3, yo, k1, yo, k3—9 sts. *6* K4, yo, k1, yo, k4—11 sts. *8* K1, ssk, k2, yo, k1, yo, k5—12 sts. *10, 12* K1, ssk, k to end. *14, 16, 18* K1, SK2P, k to end. *20* K1, SK2P—2 sts. *21* P2tog.

BALL-WINDING ANGEL LEFT WING CHART
BEGIN ON 5 STS

Row 1 and all WS rows (except 21) Purl. *2* K2, yo, k1, yo, k2—7 sts. *4* K3, yo, k1, yo, k3—9 sts. *6* K4, yo, k1, yo, k4—11 sts. *8* K5, yo, k1, yo, k2, k2tog, k1—12 sts. *10, 12* K to last 3 sts,

k2tog, k1. *14, 16, 18* K to last 4 sts, k3tog, k1. *20* K3tog, k1—2 sts. *21* P2tog.

BALL-WINDING ANGEL BODICE CHART
BEGIN ON 7 STS

Row 1 and all WS rows Purl. *2* K3, yo, k1, yo, k3—9 sts. *4, 6, 8, 10, 12* K3, yo, ssk, yo, k to end. *14, 16* Knit. *18* K3, ssk, k4, k2tog, k3—12 sts. *20* K3, ssk, k2, k2tog, k3—10 sts. *22* K3, ssk, k2tog, k3—8 sts. *23* Purl.

BALL-WINDING ANGEL SKIRT CHART
4 TO 12-ST REPEAT

Rnd 1 and all odd-numbered rnds Knit. *2* *Yo, ssk, yo, k2; rep from*—20 sts. *4* *Yo, ssk, yo, k3; rep from*—24 sts. *6* *Yo, ssk, yo, k4; rep from*—28 sts. *8* *Yo, ssk, yo, k5; rep from*—32 sts. *10* *Yo, ssk, yo, k6; rep from*—36 sts. *12* *[Yo, k1] 3 times, yo, ssk, k2, k2tog; rep from*—44 sts. *14* *Yo, k3, yo, k1, yo, k3, yo, ssk, k2tog; rep from*—52 sts. *16* *Yo, ssk, k7, k2tog, yo, ssk; rep from*—48 sts. *18* *K1, yo, ssk, k5, k2tog, yo, k2; rep from*. *20* *K2, yo, ssk, k3, k2tog, yo, k3; rep from*. *22* *K3, yo, ssk, k1, k2tog, yo, k4; rep from*. *24* *K4, yo, S2KP2, yo, k5; rep from*. *25* Knit.

K on RS, p on WS
P on RS, k on WS
K into front & back of st
Yo
S2KP2
SK2P
K3tog
Ssk on RS, ssp on WS
K2tog on RS, p2tog on WS
1/1 RT
1/1 LT

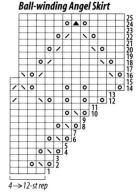

Ball-winding Angel Skirt

4→12-st rep

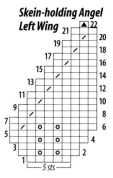

Skein-holding Angel Left Wing

5 sts

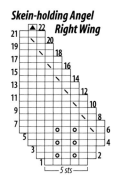

Skein-holding Angel Right Wing

5 sts

SKEIN-HOLDING ANGEL RIGHT WING CHART
BEGIN ON 5 STS

Row 1 and all WS rows Purl. **2** K2, yo, k1, yo, k2—7 sts. **4** K3, yo, k1, yo, k3—9 sts. **6** K1, ssk, [k1, yo] twice, k4—10 sts. **8, 10, 12, 14, 16, 18, 20** K1, ssk, k to end. **22** S2KP2.

SKEIN-HOLDING ANGEL LEFT WING CHART
BEGIN ON 5 STS

Row 1 and all WS rows Purl. **2** K2, yo, k1, yo, k2—7 sts. **4** K3, yo, k1, yo, k3—9 sts. **6** K4, [yo, k1] twice, k2tog, k1—10 sts. **8, 10, 12, 14, 16, 18, 20** K to last 3 sts, k2tog, k1. **22** S2KP2.

SKEIN-HOLDING ANGEL BODICE CHART
BEGIN ON 7 STS

Row 1 and all WS rows (except 17 and 19) K1, p to last st, k1. **2, 4, 6** K1, k into front and back of st, k to last 3 sts, k into front and back of st, k2. **8, 10** Knit. **12, 14, 16** K1, ssk, k3, yo, k1, yo, k3, k2tog, k1. **17** K1, p2tog, p7, ssp, k1—11 sts. **18** K1, 1/1 LT, k5, 1/1 RT, k1. **19** K1, p1, p2tog, p3, ssp, p1, k1—9 sts. **20** K2, 1/1 LT, k1, 1/1 RT, k2. **22** K3, SK2P, k3—7 sts. **23** Rep row 1.

SKEIN-HOLDING ANGEL SKIRT CHART
4 TO 12-ST REPEAT

Rnd 1 and all odd-numbered rnds Knit. **2** *[K1, yo] twice, k2; rep from*—24 sts. **4** *K2, yo, k1, yo, k3; rep from*—32 sts. **6** *K3, yo, k1, yo, k4; rep from*—40 sts. **8** *Ssk, k7, yo, k1, yo; rep from*—44 sts. **10** *Ssk, k6, yo, ssk, yo, k1; rep from*. **12** *Ssk, k5, [yo, ssk] twice, yo; rep from*. **14** *Ssk, k4, [yo, ssk] twice, yo, k1; rep from*. **16** *Ssk, k3, [yo, ssk] 3 times, yo; rep from*. **18** *Ssk, k2, [yo, ssk] 3 times, yo, k1; rep from*. **20** *Ssk, k1, [yo, ssk] 4 times, yo; rep from*. **22** *[Ssk, yo] 5 times, k1; rep from*. **24** *K1, [yo, ssk] 5 times, yo; rep from*—48 sts. **25** Knit.

Skein-holding Angel Bodice

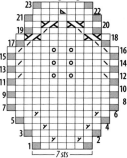

7 sts

Skein-holding Angel Skirt

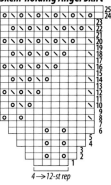

4→12-st rep

Ball-winding Angel Bodice

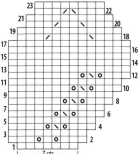

7 sts

13

Angels make great gifts for all our fiber-artist friends. Here, one hooks a rug while the other is busy spinning. (And what would an angel spin? Gold thread of course.) The rug-hooking angel is knitted in the ground lace pattern known as English Mesh or Busy Bees.

Rug-hooking Angel

SIZE
3½" high

YARN
Coats & Clark • Knit-Cro-Sheen
100% cotton • 225yds/205m
1 ball

NEEDLES
2.25mm/US1
double-pointed needles (dpn)
Set of 4

EXTRAS
Cornstarch • Tapestry needle
Polyester fiberfill or cotton ball
White clear-drying glue

RUG-HOOKING ANGEL
Two ¾" gold or silver plastic rings
(wedding supply)
Small piece of unbleached muslin
Small amount of darning wool
¾" piece of #22 or #24 florist's wire
Small gold oval bead

14

Notes 1 See *School*, p. 50 for ssk, M1, lifted increase, SK2P, and S2KP2. **2** Arms, Wings, and Bodice are worked back and forth with 2 dpn. Head and Skirt are worked circularly. **3** In Canada: Use Coats & Clark's "Mercerized" (1,000m ball). **4** Charts are on pages 18–19.

RUG-HOOKING ANGEL
Arms *MAKE 2*
Cast on 7 sts. Work 20 rows of Arms Chart. Fasten off last st.
Wings *MAKE 2*
Cast on 7 sts. Work 16 rows of Rug-hooking Angel Wing Chart. Fasten off last st.
Bodice
Cast on 7 sts. Work 20 rows of Rug-hooking Angel Bodice Chart. Bind off remaining 7 sts.
Skirt
Cast on 48 sts and divide evenly onto 3 dpn (18-18-12). **Rnd 1** Work 6-st repeat of Rug-hooking Angel Skirt Chart 8 times. Continue in chart pattern through rnd 24. Bind off remaining 16 sts.
Head
Cast on 9 sts and divide evenly onto 3 dpn. **Rnds 1 and 3** Knit. **2** *K1, lifted increase into 2nd st, k1; repeat from*—12 sts. **4** *K1, lifted increase into 2nd st; repeat from*—18 sts. **5–8** Knit. **9** *K1, ssk; repeat from*—12 sts. **10 and 12** Knit. **11** *K1, ssk, k1; repeat from*—9 sts. Cut yarn and pull through remaining loops. Do not pull tightly.
Finishing
Use two ¾" gold or silver plastic rings for hoops. Cut one ring and remove approximately ⅜" for inner hoop. Cut 1½" square of unbleached muslin for 'rug backing'. With darning wool, embroider small motif (flower, holly, etc.) on muslin, using backstitch. Insert muslin between rings and secure with clear glue. Bend one end of florist's wire into a hook. Glue oval bead to other end for handle. See Both Angels on next page for remaining finishing.

Back stitch

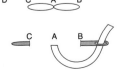

Spinning Angel

Notes *1* See *School*, p. 50 for ssk, ssp, SK2P, S2KP2, and lifted increase. *2* Arms, Wings, and Bodice are worked back and forth with 2 dpn. Head and Skirt are worked circularly. *3* In Canada: Use Coats & Clark's "Mercerized" (1,000m ball). *4* See page 18-19 for charts.

SPINNING ANGEL *5 RIB*
Arms *MAKE 2*
Cast on 7 sts. Work 20 rows of Arms Chart. Fasten off last st.
Right wing
Cast on 5 sts. Work 24 rows of Spinning Angel Right Wing Chart. Fasten off last st.
Left wing
Cast on 5 sts. Work 24 rows of Spinning Angel Left Wing Chart. Fasten off last st.
Bodice
Cast on 7 sts. Work 21 rows of Spinning Angel Bodice Chart. Bind off remaining 7 sts.
Skirt
Cast on 50 sts and divide onto 3 dpn (20-10-20). **Rnd 1** Work 10-st repeat of Spinning Angel Skirt Chart 5 times. Continue in chart pattern through rnd 24—20 sts. **Rnd 25** *K1, k2tog; repeat from*, binding off as you go.

Head
Cast on 9 sts evenly onto 3 dpn. **Rnds 1 and 3** Knit. **2** *K1, lifted increase into 2nd st, k1; repeat from*—12 sts. **4** *K1, lifted increase into 2nd st; repeat from*—18 sts. **5–8** Knit. **9** *K1, ssk; repeat from*—12 sts. **10 and 12** Knit. **11** *K1, ssk, k1; repeat from*—9 sts. Cut yarn and pull through remaining loops. Do not pull tightly.

Finishing
Make 'drop spindle': Shorten toothpick to 1¾" and paint desired color. Push flat bead or 2 sequins ¼" up from bottom. Wind 6" of metallic yarn around spindle above bead. Secure with half hitch and glue. Unravel remaining yarn to make 'fibers' for spinning.

BOTH ANGELS
Darn in ends at lower edge of skirt and tips of wings before stiffening. Use other ends for joining pieces and to hold accessories. See *How to Assemble and Angel*, page 46.

Using photo on page 17 as guide, use yarn at end of hands to hold accessories.

SIZE
3½" high

YARN
Coats & Clark • Knit-Cro-Sheen
100% cotton • 225yds/205m
1 ball

NEEDLES
2.25mm/US 1
double-pointed needles (dpn)
Set of 4

EXTRAS
Cornstarch • Tapestry needle
Polyester fiberfill or cotton ball
White clear-drying glue
Round wooden toothpick
¼" flat bead or two 5mm cup-
shaped sequins
12" gold metallic yarn • Paint

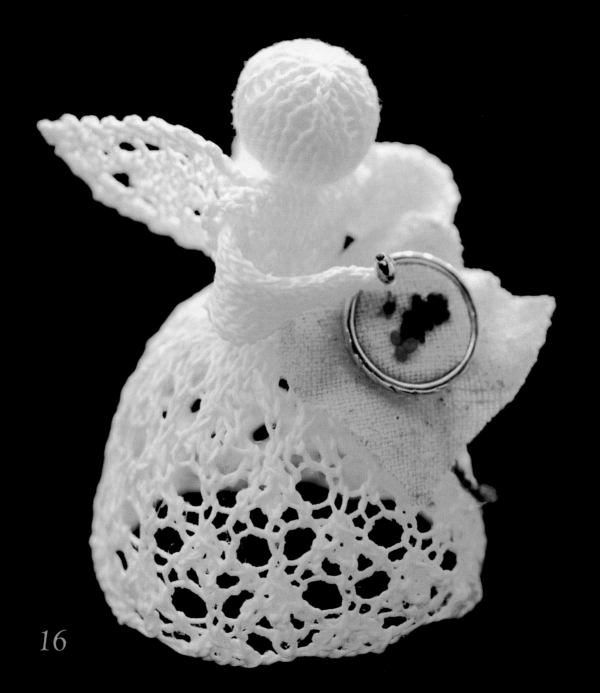

16

17

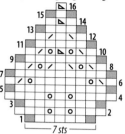

Rug-hooking Angel Wings

7 sts

Arms

7 sts

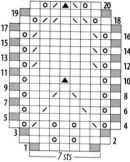

Rug-hooking Angel Bodice

7 sts

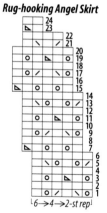

Rug-hooking Angel Skirt

6→4→2-st rep

in other words...

ARMS CHART
BEGIN ON 7 STS
Row 1 and all WS rows K1, p to last st, k1. **2, 4, and 6** K into front and back of st, k to last 2 sts, k into front and back of st, k1. **8** Knit—13 sts. **10** K4, k2tog, k1, ssk, k4. **12** K3, k2tog, k1, ssk, k3. **14** K2, k2tog, k1, ssk, k2. **16** K1, k2tog, k1, ssk, k1. **18** K2tog, k1, ssk—3 sts. **20** SK2P.

RUG-HOOKING ANGEL WING CHART
BEGIN ON 7 STS
Row 1 and all WS rows K1, p to last st, k1. **2** K3, yo, k1, yo, k3—9 sts. **4** K4, yo, k1, yo, k4—11 sts. **6** K1, ssk, yo, k5, yo, k2tog, k1. **8** K1, ssk, yo, ssk, k1, k2tog, yo, k2tog, k1—9 sts. **10** K1, ssk, yo, SK2P, yo, k2tog, k1—7 sts. **12** K1, ssk, k1, k2tog, k1—5 sts. **14** K1, SK2P, k1—3 sts. **16** SK2P.

RUG-HOOKING ANGEL BODICE CHART
BEGIN ON 7 STS
Row 1 and all WS rows K1, p to last st, k1. **2** K3, yo, k1, yo, k3—9 sts. **4** K1, yo, ssk, [k1, yo] twice, k1, k2tog, yo, k1—11 sts. **6** K1, yo, k1, ssk, k3, k2tog, k1, yo, k1. **8** K1, yo, k2, ssk, k1, k2tog, k2, yo, k1. **10** K1, yo, k3, S2KP3, k3, yo, k1. **12, 14, and 16** K1, yo, ssk, k5, k2tog, yo, k1. **18** K1, yo, [ssk] twice, k1, [k2tog] twice, yo, k1—9 sts. **20** K1, yo, ssk, S2KP2, k2tog, yo, k1—7 sts.

RUG-HOOKING ANGEL SKIRT CHART
6 TO 4 TO 2-ST REPEAT
Note Before working chart rnds 7, 15, and 23, slip first st of each dpn to become the last st of previous dpn.
Rnd 1 *Yo, ssk, k1, k2tog, yo, k1; rep from*. **2 and all even-numbered rnds** Knit. **3** *Yo, k1, SK2P, k1, yo, k1; rep from*. **5** *K2tog, yo, k1, yo, ssk, k1; rep from*. **7** See Note above. *[K1, yo] twice, k1, SK2P; rep from*. **9–15** Rep rnds 1–7. **17–19** Rep rnds 1–3. **21** *K2tog, k1, ssk, k1; rep from*—32 sts. **23** See Note above. *K1, SK2P; rep from*—16 sts. **24** Knit.

18

- ☐ K on RS, p on WS
- ■ P on RS, k on WS
- ◿ Ssk on RS, ssp on WS
- ◿ K2tog on RS, p2tog on WS
- ⊙ Yo
- ◣ SK2P ▲ S2KP2
- ◢ K3tog ◢ P3tog
- ☒ K into front and back of st
- ☒ P into front and back of st
- ⊙⊙ Yo twice

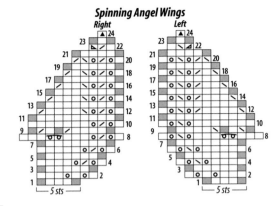

Spinning Angel Wings
Right   Left

SPINNING ANGEL RIGHT WING CHART
BEGIN ON 5 STS

Row 1 and all WS rows (except 9) K1, p to last st, k1. **2** [K1, yo] twice, k3—7 sts. **4** K1, yo, k2tog, yo, k4—8 sts. **6** K1, yo, k2tog, yo, k5—9 sts. **8** K1, yo, k2tog, yo, k3, yo twice, k3—12 sts. **9** (WS) K1, p2tog, p1 into first yo, k1 into 2nd yo, p2tog, p4, k1—10 sts. **10** K1, yo, k2tog, yo, k7—11 sts. **12, 14, 16, 18** K1, yo, k2tog, yo, ssk, k to last 2 sts, k2tog. **20** K1, yo, k2tog, yo, ssk, k2tog—6 sts. **22** K1, k2tog, SK2P—3 sts. **24** S2KP2.

SPINNING ANGEL LEFT WING CHART
BEGIN ON 5 STS

Row 1 and all WS rows (except 9) K1, p to last st, k1. **2** K3, [yo, k1] twice—7 sts. **4** K4, yo, ssk, yo, k1—8 sts. **6** K5, yo, ssk, yo, k1—9 sts. **8** K3, yo twice, k3, yo, ssk, yo, k1—12 sts. **9** (WS) K1, p4, ssp, k1 into first yo, p1 into 2nd yo, ssp, k1—10 sts. **10** K7, yo, ssk, yo, k1—11 sts. **12, 14, 16, 18** Ssk, k to last 5 sts, k2tog, yo, ssk, yo, k1. **20** Ssk, k2tog, yo, ssk, yo, k1—6 sts. **22** K3tog, ssk, k1—3 sts. **24** S2KP2.

SPINNING ANGEL BODICE CHART
BEGIN ON 7 STS

Row 1 and all WS rows K1, p to last st, k1. **2** K1, yo, k into front and back of st, p2, p into front and back of st, k1, yo, k1—11 sts. **4** K1, yo, k3, p3, k3, yo, k1—13 sts. **6, 8, 10, 12, 14, 16** K1, yo, k2, k2tog, p3, ssk, k2, yo, k1. **18** K1, yo, ssk, k2tog, p3, ssk, k2tog, yo, k1—11 sts. **20** K1, yo, k3tog, p3tog, SK2P, yo, k1—7 sts. **21** Rep row 1.

SPINNING ANGEL SKIRT CHART
10 TO 4-ST REP

Rnd 1 *P1, ssk, k2, yo, k1, yo, k2, k2tog; rep from*. **2 and all even-numbered rnds** Knit. **3–17 (odd-numbered rnds)** Rep rnd 1. **19** *P1, SK2P, k1, [yo, k1] twice, k3tog; rep from*—40 sts. **21** *P1, SK2P, yo, k1, yo, k3tog; rep from*—30 sts. **23** *P1, ssk, k1, k2tog; rep from *—20 sts. **24** Knit.

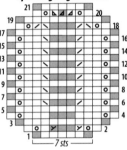

Spinning Angel Bodice

7 sts

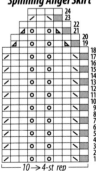

Spinning Angel Skirt

10 → 4-st rep

19

My next angel crochets a gold halo with her left hand. Both the crocheting and spinning angels' skirts are knit from the bottom up in the Shetland pattern known as Razor Shell. These skirts are narrower, and mold well over a styrofoam egg.

7 Crocheting Angel

SIZE
3½" high

YARN
Coats & Clark · Knit-Cro-Sheen
100% cotton · 225yds/205m
1 ball

NEEDLES
2.25mm/US 1
double-pointed needles (dpn)
Set of 4

EXTRAS
Cornstarch · Tapestry needle
Polyester fiberfill or cotton ball
White clear-drying glue
22 and 24 gauge brass wire
2 bugle beads
2 yds gold metallic yarn
Crochet hook of comparable size

Notes 1 See *School*, p. 50 for ssk, ssp, SK2P, S2KP2, and lifted increase. **2** Arms, Wings, and Bodice are worked back and forth with 2 dpn. Head and Skirt are worked circularly. **3** In Canada: Use Coats & Clark's "Mercerized" (1,000m ball). **4** See page 24 for charts.

CROCHETING ANGEL *6 RIB*
Arms *MAKE 2*
Cast on 7 sts. Work 20 rows of Arms Chart. Fasten off last st.
Wings *MAKE 2*
Cast on 7 sts. Work rows 1–6 of Crocheting Angel Wing Chart. ***Divide wing: Right half row 7*** (RS) Work first 7 sts of chart, turn. Work through chart row 14 on these 7 sts. Cut yarn 24" long and pull end through remaining loop. With tapestry needle, pull end through edge 'nubs' on WS of wing to bring yarn into position to resume knitting on remaining sts. Follow chart and work left half of wing. Fasten off.
Bodice
Cast on 7 sts. Work 21 rows of Crocheting Angel Bodice Chart. Bind off remaining 7 sts.

Skirt
Cast on 48 sts and divide evenly onto 3 dpn. **Rnd 1** Work 8-st rep of Crocheting Angel Skirt Chart 6 times. Continue in chart pattern through rnd 22—36 sts. **Rnd 23** K2tog, *SK2P; rep from* to last st. Sl last st over st on first dpn. **Rnd 24** Knit. Bind off.
Head
Cast on 9 sts and divide evenly onto 3 dpn. Rnds 1 and 3 Knit. 2 *K1, lifted increase into 2nd st, k1; rep from*—12 sts. 4 *K1, lifted increase into 2nd st; rep from*—18 sts. 5–8 Knit. 9 *K1, ssk; rep from*—12 sts. 10 and 12 Knit. 11 *K1, ssk, k1; rep from*—9 sts. Cut yarn and pull through remaining loops. Do not pull tightly.
Finishing
Use finer-gauge brass wire for 'crochet hook'. Cut wire approx ¾" long. Bend end to make hook. Slide and glue 2 bugle beads on other end for 'handle'. With metallic yarn, crochet a chain approximately 2½" long for halo. Cut yarn, leaving a 1 yd tail. Tie a knot in end, then wind into tiny ball, ending with 2 half hitches. Secure with glue. Make a ¾" diameter ring of heavier-gauge wire. Weave wire in and out of crocheted chain to stiffen halo. See Both Angels, page 22, for remaining finishing.

21

This angel is weaving on the strings of her harp. Her skirt is adapted from the Waterfall pattern in The Treasury of Knitting *by Barbara Walker.*

8 Weaving Angel

SIZE
3½" high

YARN
Coats & Clark · Knit-Cro-Sheen
100% cotton · 225yds/205m
1 ball

NEEDLES
2.25mm/US1
double-pointed needles (dpn)
Set of 4

EXTRAS
Cornstarch · Tapestry needle
Polyester fiberfill or cotton ball
White clear-drying glue

WEAVING ANGEL
Pull tab (square at the wide end)
from aluminum drink can
Tin snips and file · Gold paint
Fine crochet or sewing thread

Notes See Notes for Crocheting Angel, page 20.

WEAVING ANGEL
Arms *MAKE 2*
Cast on 7 sts. Work 20 rows of Arms Chart. Fasten off last st.
Right Wing
Cast on 5 sts. Work 14 rows of Weaving Angel Right Wing Chart. Fasten off last st.
Left Wing
Cast on 5 sts. Work 14 rows of Weaving Angel Left Wing Chart. Fasten off last st.
Bodice
Cast on 7 sts. Work 23 rows of Weaving Angel Bodice Chart. Bind off remaining 7 sts.
Skirt
Cast on 48 sts and divide evenly onto 3 dpn. *Rnd 1* Work 8-st repeat of Weaving Angel Skirt Chart 6 times. Continue in chart pattern through rnd 22—36 sts. *Rnd 23* K2tog, *k1, p1, k1, SK2P; repeat from* to last 4 sts, k1, p1, k1, slip 1, pass slip st over k2tog on first dpn—24 sts. *Rnd 24* *K1, SK2P; repeat from*. Bind off remaining 12 sts.
Head
Cast on 9 sts and divide evenly onto 3 dpn. *Rnds 1 and 3* Knit. *2* *K1, lifted increase into

2nd st, k1; repeat from*—12 sts. *4* *K1, lifted increase into 2nd st; repeat from*—18 sts. *5–8* Knit. *9* *K1, ssk; repeat from*—12 sts. *10 and 12* Knit. *11* *K1, ssk, k1; repeat from*—9 sts. Cut yarn and pull through remaining loops. Do not pull tightly.
Finishing
With tin snips, cut from wide corners of pull tab toward center, removing top section. File ragged edges. Paint with gold paint. Wind fine crochet cotton or sewing thread approx 8 times around 2 horizontal bars for 'warp'. Use ends to weave approximately 6 shots through warp. Cut beginning thread when fastened in; wind 'butterfly' from other end, leaving approximately 2" between weaving and 'butterfly'. (To wind butterfly, with 6" end, wind a tiny skein, wind end around center to hold.)

BOTH ANGELS
Darn in ends at lower edge of skirt and tips of wings before stiffening. Use other ends for joining pieces and to hold accessories. See *How to Assemble an Angel*, page 46.
Using photo as guide, use yarn at end of hands to hold accessories.

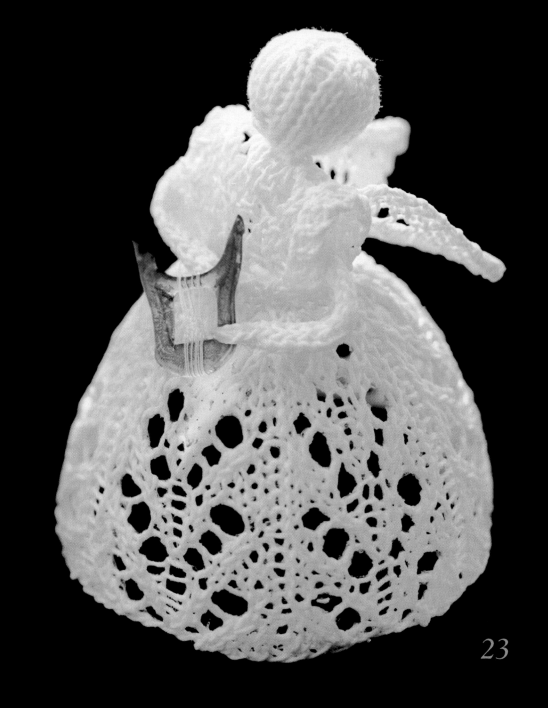

23

Crocheting Angel Bodice

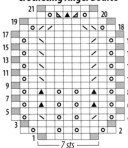

Crocheting Angel Wing

Arms

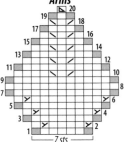

Crocheting Angel Skirt

in other words…

ARMS CHART
BEGIN ON 7 STS

Row 1 and all WS rows K1, p to last st, k1. ***2, 4, and 6*** K into front and back of st, k to last 2 sts, k into front and back of st, k1. ***8*** Knit— 13 sts. ***10*** K4, k2tog, k1, ssk, k4. ***12*** K3, k2tog, k1, ssk, k3. ***14*** K2, k2tog, k1, ssk, k2. ***16*** K1, k2tog, k1, ssk, k1. ***18*** K2tog, k1, ssk—3 sts. ***20*** SK2P.

CROCHETING ANGEL WING CHART
BEGIN ON 7 STS

Row 1 (RS) K1, [yo, k2, yo, k1] twice—11 sts. ***2, 4, and 6*** K1, p to last st, k1. ***3*** K1, yo, k1, k2tog, yo, k3, yo, ssk, k1, yo, k1—13 sts. ***5*** K1, yo, k1, k2tog, yo, k5, yo, ssk, k1, yo, k1—15 sts. ***Right Half: Rows 7 and 9*** K1, [yo, k1, k2tog] twice, turn—7 sts. ***8, 10, and 12*** P to last st, k1. ***11*** K1, [yo, k3tog] twice, turn—5 sts. ***13*** K3tog, k2tog—2 sts. ***14*** P2tog. ***Left Half: Row 7*** S2KP2, k1, yo, ssk, k1, yo, k1—7 sts. ***8, 10 and 12*** K1, p to end. ***9*** [Ssk, k1, yo] twice, k1. ***11*** [SK2P, yo] twice, k1—5 sts. ***13*** Ssk, SK2P—2 sts. ***14*** Ssp.

CROCHETING ANGEL BODICE CHART
BEGIN ON 7 STS

Row 1 and all WS rows K1, p to last st, k1. ***2*** [K1, yo, k2, yo] twice, k1—11 sts. ***4*** K1, yo, k1, k2tog, k1, [yo, k1] twice, ssk, k1, yo, k1—13 sts. ***6 and 8*** [K1, yo, k1, S2KP2, k1, yo] twice, k1. ***10, 12, 14, 16*** K1, yo, k1, k2tog, k5, ssk, k1, yo, k1. ***18*** K1, yo, [ssk] twice, k3, [k2tog] twice, yo, k1—11 sts. ***20*** K1, yo, k3tog, S2KP2, SK2P, yo, k1—7 sts. ***21*** Rep row 1.

CROCHETING ANGEL SKIRT CHART
8 TO 6-ST REP

Rnd 1 *P1, ssk, k1, [yo, k1] twice, k2tog; rep from*. ***2*** Knit. ***3–20*** Rep rnds 1–2. ***21*** *P1, SK2P, yo, k1, yo, k3tog; rep from*—36 sts. ***22*** Knit.

24

Weaving Angel Left Wing

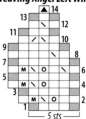

Weaving Angel Right Wing

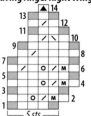

Key:
- ☐ K on RS, p on WS
- ▨ P on RS, k on WS
- ⊠ K into front and back of st
- ⊙ Yo
- ◺ Ssk
- ◿ K2tog
- ◸ SK2P
- ▲ S2K2P
- Ⓜ M1

Weaving Angel Bodice

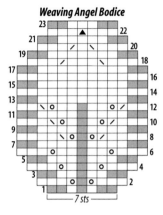

Weaving Angel Skirt

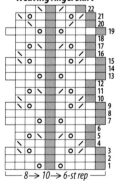

WEAVING ANGEL RIGHT WING CHART
BEGIN ON 5 STS

Row 1 and all WS rows K1, p to last st, k1.
2 K1, M1, k2tog, yo, k2—6 sts. **4** K1, M1, k2tog, yo, k3—7 sts. **6** K1, M1, k2tog, yo, k1, k2tog, k1. **8** K4, k2tog, k1—6 sts. **10** K1, ssk, k2tog, k1—4 sts. **12** K1, k2tog, k1—3 sts. **14** S2K2P2.

WEAVING ANGEL LEFT WING CHART
BEGIN ON 5 STS

Row 1 and all WS rows K1, p to last st, k1.
 2 K2, yo, ssk, M1, k1—6 sts. **4** K3, yo, ssk, M1, k1—7 sts. **6** K1, ssk, k1, yo, ssk, M1, k1. **8** K1, ssk, k4—6 sts. **10** K1, ssk, k2tog, k1—4 sts. **12** K1, ssk, k1—3 sts. **14** S2K2P2.

WEAVING ANGEL BODICE CHART
BEGIN ON 7 STS

Row 1 (WS) K2, p1, k1, p1, k2. **2** K3, yo, p1, yo, k3—9 sts. **3** K2, p2, k1, p2, k2. **4** K3, yo, k1, p1, k1, yo, k3—11 sts. **5** K2, p3, k1, p3, k2. **6** K3, yo, k2, p1, k2, yo, k3—13 sts. **7, 9, 11** K2, p4, k1, p4, k2. **8** K4, k2tog, yo, p1, yo, ssk, k4. **10** K3, k2tog, yo, k1, p1, k1, yo, ssk, k3. **12** K2, k2tog, yo, k2, p1, k2, yo, ssk, k2. **13 and all following WS rows** K2, p to last 2 sts, k2. **14, 16** Knit. **18** K3, ssk, k3, k2tog, k3—11 sts. **20** K3, ssk, k1, k2tog, k3—9 sts. **22** K3, S2KP2, k3—7 sts. **23** Rep row 11.

WEAVING ANGEL SKIRT CHART
8 TO 10 TO 6-ST REPEAT

Rnd 1 *P1, k3, yo, p1, yo, k3; rep from*—60 sts. **2** *P1, k4; rep from*. **3** *P1, k1, k2tog, yo, k1, p1, k1, yo, ssk, k1; rep from*. **4** *P1, k2tog, k2, p1, k2, ssk; rep from*—48 sts. **5** *P1, k1, yo, k2tog, p1, ssk, yo, k1; rep from*. **6** *P1, k3; rep from*. **7–18** Rep rnds 1–6 twice. **19** Rep rnd 1—60 sts. **20** *P1, k1, k2tog, k1, p1, k1, ssk, k1; rep from*—48 sts. **21** *P1, k2tog, yo, k1, p1, k1, yo, ssk; rep from*. **22** *P1, k1, k2tog, p1, ssk, k1; rep from*—36 sts.

The Ladybird stitch used on this angel's skirt is a lace pattern from Marianne Kinzel's First Book of Modern Lace Knitting.

9 Embroidering Angel

SIZE
3½" high

YARN
Coats & Clark • Knit-Cro-Sheen
100% cotton • 225yds/205m
1 ball

NEEDLES
2.25mm/US1
double-pointed needles (dpn)
Set of 4

EXTRAS BOTH
Cornstarch • Tapestry needle
Polyester fiberfill or cotton ball
White clear-drying glue
EMBROIDERING ANGEL
Two ¾" gold or silver plastic rings
(wedding supply)
Small piece of lightweight petit
point mesh fabric
Small amount of red embroidery
floss
QUILTING ANGEL
Several colors of metallic ribbon
Small piece of fusible web backing

Notes 1 See *School,* page 50 for ssk, M1, lifted increase, SK2P, and S2KP2. **2** Arms, Wings, and Bodice are worked back and forth with 2 dpn. Head and Skirt are worked circularly. **3** In Canada: Use Coats & Clark's "Mercerized" (1,000m ball). **4** Charts are on pages 30-31.

EMBROIDERING ANGEL
Arms *MAKE 2*
Cast on 7 sts. Work 20 rows of Arms Chart. Fasten off last st.
Wings *MAKE 2*
Cast on 7 sts. Work 16 rows of Embroidering Angel Wing Chart. Fasten off last st.
Bodice
Cast on 9 sts. Work 23 rows of Embroidering Angel Bodice Chart. Bind off remaining 7 sts.
Skirt
Cast on 54 sts and divide evenly onto 3 dpn. ***Rnd 1*** Work 6-st repeat of Embroidering Angel Skirt Chart 9 times. Continue in chart pattern through rnd 24. Bind off remaining 18 sts.
Head
Cast on 9 sts and divide evenly onto 3 dpn.

Rnds 1, 3 Knit. **2** *K1, lifted increase into 2nd st, k1; repeat from*—12 sts. **4** *K1, lifted increase into second st; repeat from*—18 sts. **5–8** Knit. **9** *K1, ssk; repeat from*—12 sts. **10, 12** Knit. **11** *K1, ssk, k1; repeat from*—9 sts. Cut yarn and pull through remaining loops. Do not pull tightly.
Finishing
Use two ¾" gold or silver plastic rings for hoops. Cut one ring and remove approximately ⅜" for inner hoop. Embroider small heart motif (or holly sprig, "joy", or initials) on lightweight petit point mesh fabric with single strand of embroidery cotton. Insert mesh between rings and secure with clear glue. See Both Angels , page 28, for remaining finishing.

Embroidery diagram

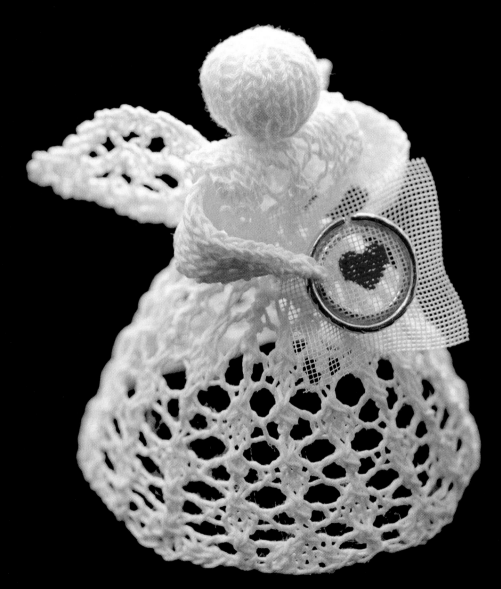

27

The quilting angel's skirt is knit in Vine Lace, a pattern found in Barbara Walker's A Treasury of Knitting Patterns.

Quilting Angel

Notes See Embroidering Angel, page 26 for Size, Yarn, Needles, Extras, and Notes.

QUILTING ANGEL
Arms *MAKE 2*

Cast on 7 sts. Work 20 rows of Arms Chart. Fasten off last st.

Quilting diagram

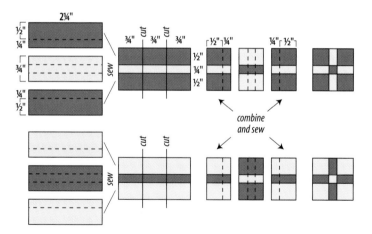

combine
and sew

Key
- - - - Seamline

Right Wing

Cast on 6 sts. Work 20 rows of Quilting Angel Right Wing Chart. Fasten off last st.
Left Wing

Cast on 6 sts. Work 20 rows of Quilting Angel Left Wing Chart. Fasten off last st.

Bodice

Cast on 8 sts. Work 22 rows of Quilting Angel Bodice Chart. Bind off remaining 8 sts.
Skirt

Cast on 54 sts and divide evenly onto 3 dpn. ***Rnd 1*** Work 9-st repeat of Quilting Angel Skirt Chart 6 times. Continue in chart pattern through rnd 22—42 sts. ***Rnd 23*** K2tog, *ssk, k2tog, SK2P; repeat from* to last 5 sts, ssk, k2tog, slip 1, pass slip st over k2tog on first dpn—18 sts. ***Rnd 24*** Knit. Bind off.
Head

Cast on 9 sts and divide evenly onto 3 dpn. ***Rnds 1, 3*** Knit. ***2*** *K1, lifted increase into 2nd st, k1; repeat from*—12 sts. ***4*** *K1, lifted increase into second st; repeat from*—18 sts. ***5–8*** Knit. ***9*** *K1, ssk; repeat from*—12 sts. ***10, 12*** Knit. ***11*** *K1, ssk, k1; repeat from*—9 sts. Cut yarn and pull through remaining loops. Do not pull tightly.
Finishing

Make 1¼" patchwork square using 2 metallic ribbons and strip piecing techniques (Seminole patchwork). It is easier to make several units and cut them apart, combining the most interesting units (see diagram). Use fusible web backing.

(continues on page 30)

Embroidering Angel Wing

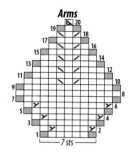

Arms

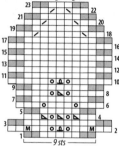

Embroidering Angel Bodice

Embroidering Angel Skirt

(continued from page 28)

BOTH ANGELS

Weave in ends at lower edge of skirt and tips of wings before stiffening. Use other ends for joining pieces and to hold accessories. See *How to Assemble an Angel*, page 46.

Using photo as guide, use yarn at end of hands to hold accessories.

in other words...

ARMS CHART
BEGIN ON 7 STS

Row 1 and all WS rows K1, p to last st, k1. **2, 4, and 6** K into front and back of st, k to last 2 sts, k into front and back of st, k1. **8** Knit—13 sts. **10** K4, k2tog, k1, ssk, k4. **12** K3, k2tog, k1, ssk, k3. **14** K2, k2tog, k1, ssk, k2. **16** K1, k2tog, k1, ssk, k1. **18** K2tog, k1, ssk—3 sts. **20** SK2P.

EMBROIDERING ANGEL WING CHART
BEGIN ON 7 STS

Row 1 and all WS rows K1, p to last st, k1. **2** K1, M1, k2, yo, k1 tbl, yo, k2, M1, k1—11 sts. **4** K1, M1, SK2P, [yo, SK2P] twice, M1, k1—9 sts. **6** [K3, yo] twice, k3—11 sts. **8** K1, SK2P,

[yo, SK2P] twice, k1—7 sts. **10** K1, ssk, yo, k1 tbl, yo, k2tog, k1. **12** K1, ssk, k1, k2tog, k1—5 sts. **14** K1, S2KP2, k1—3 sts. **16** S2KP2.

EMBROIDERY ANGEL BODICE CHART
BEGIN ON 9 STS

Row 1 and all WS rows K2, p to last 2 sts, k2. **2** K2, M1, k2, yo, k1 tbl, yo, k2, M1, k2—13 sts. **4** K2, SK2P, [yo, SK2P] twice, k2—9 sts. **6** [K3, yo] twice, k3—11 sts. **8** K4, yo, SK2P, yo, k4. **10** K5, yo, k1 tbl, yo, k5—13 sts. **12, 14, and 16** Knit. **18** K2, ssk, k5, k2tog, k2—11 sts. **20** K2, ssk, k3, k2tog, k2—9 sts. **22** K2, ssk, k1, k2tog, k2—7 sts. **23** Rep row 1.

EMBROIDERING ANGEL SKIRT CHART
6 TO 4 TO 2-ST REPEAT

Rnd 1 and all odd-numbered rnds Knit. **2** *Yo, k1 tbl, yo, ssk, k1, k2tog; rep from*. **4** *Yo, SK2P; rep from*—36 sts. **6** *K3, yo, k1tbl, yo; rep from*—54 sts. **8** *SK2P, yo; rep from*—36 sts. **10** *Yo, k1 tbl, yo, k3; rep from*—54 sts. **12–18** Rep rows 4–10. **20** Rep rnd 4—36 sts. **22** *SK2P, yo, k1 tbl, yo; rep from*. **24** *K1, SK2P; rep from*—18 sts.

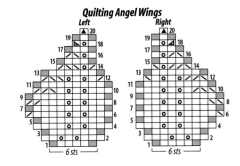

Quilting Angel Wings

Left   Right

Legend:

☐ K on RS, p on WS ▧ P on RS, k on WS   ○ Yo   Ⓜ M1   ◩ Ssk ◪ K2tog   ◨ SK2P ◲ K3tog   ▲ S2KP2   ◩ K1 through back loop (tbl) ⊠ K into front and back of st

QUILTING ANGEL RIGHT WING CHART
BEGIN ON 6 STS

Row 1 and all WS rows K1, p to last st, k1. *2* K2, yo, k1, yo, k3—8 sts. *4* K4, yo, k1, yo, k3—10 sts. *6* Ssk, k4, yo, k1, yo, k3—11 sts. *8* [Ssk] twice, k3, yo, k1, yo, k3. *10* [Ssk] twice, k2tog, [k1, yo] twice, k3—10 sts. *12* Ssk, [k2tog] twice, [yo, k1] twice, ssk—8 sts. *14* Ssk, [k2tog] twice, yo, ssk—5 sts. *16* Ssk, k2tog, yo, k1—4 sts. *18* K3tog, yo, k1—3 sts. *20* S2KP2.

QUILTING ANGEL LEFT WING CHART
BEGIN ON 6 STS

Row 1 and all WS rows K1, p to last st, k1. *2* K3, yo, k1, yo, k2—8 sts. *4* K3, yo, k1, yo, k4—10 sts. *6* K3, yo, k1, yo, k4, k2tog—11 sts. *8* K3, yo, k1, yo, k3, [k2tog] twice. *10* K3, [yo, k1] twice, ssk, [k2tog] twice—10 sts. *12* K2tog, [k1, yo] twice, [ssk] twice, k2tog—8 sts. *14* K2tog, yo, [ssk] twice, k2tog—5 sts. *16* K1, yo, ssk, k2tog—4 sts. *18* K1, yo, SK2P—3 sts. *20* S2KP2.

QUILTING ANGEL BODICE CHART
BEGIN ON 8 STS

Row 1 and all WS rows K2, p to last 2 sts, k2. *2* K3, yo, k1, yo, k4—10 sts. *4* K5, yo, k1, yo, k4—12 sts. *6* K5, yo, k1, yo, k6—14 sts. *8* K3, k2tog, k2, yo, k1, yo, k2, ssk, k2. *10* K2, k2tog, k2, yo, k1, yo, k2, ssk, k3. *12, 14, and 16* Knit. *18* K3, ssk, k4, k2tog, k3—12 sts. *20* K3, ssk, k2, k2tog, k3—10 sts. *22* K3, ssk, k2tog, k3—8 sts.

QUILTING ANGEL SKIRT CHART
9 TO 7-ST REPEAT

Rnd 1 *K1, yo, k2, ssk, k2tog, k2, yo; rep from*. *2 and all even-numbered rnds* Knit. *3* *Yo, k2, ssk, k2tog, k2, yo, k1; rep from*. *5–20* Rep rnds 1–4 four times. *21* *K1, yo, [ssk] twice, [k2tog] twice, yo; rep from*—42 sts. *22* Knit.

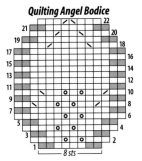

Quilting Angel Bodice

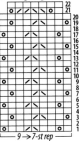

Quilting Angel Skirt

9 → 7-st rep

31

My first tree-top angel has a wide skirt and sweeping sleeves. If you wish the angels to stand, the long leaf points need to be stretched to the same length—otherwise, as my husband says, your angel will lean 'in an unholy manner.'

Traditional Angel

SIZE
9½" high

YARN
Coats & Clark Knit-Cro-Sheen
100% cotton • 225yds/205m
1 ball

NEEDLES
2.25mm/US1
double-pointed needles (dpn)
Set of 5

EXTRAS
Cornstarch
Tapestry needle
Polyester fiberfill

Notes 1 See *School,* page 50 for ssk, SSSP, lifted increase, SK2P, and S2KP2. **2** Bodice and Wings are worked back and forth with 2 dpn. Head and Arms are worked circularly; Skirts and Sleeves are worked circularly, then points are worked back and forth in rows. **3** In Canada: Use Coats & Clark's "Mercerized" (1,000m) ball. **4** Charts are on pages 37–39.

TRADITIONAL ANGEL
Bodice
Cast on 15 sts. Work 41 rows of Bodice Chart (page 37)—17 sts. Bind off all sts, working k2tog over first and last 2 sts before binding off.

Head
Cast on 12 sts and divide evenly onto 4 dpn. **Rnds 1, 3, 4** Knit. **2** *K1, lifted increase in next st, k1; repeat from*—16 sts. **5** *K1, lifted increase in next st; repeat from*—24 sts. **6, 7** Knit. **8** *K3, lifted increase in next st; repeat from*—30 sts. **9** Knit. **10** *K1, [lifted increase, k3, lifted increase, k2] twice; repeat from* once more—38 sts. **11–14** Knit. **15** *K1, [ssk, k3, ssk, k2] twice; repeat from* once more—30 sts. **16** Knit. **17** *K3, ssk; repeat from*—24 sts.

18, 19 Knit. **20** *K1, ssk; repeat from*—16 sts. **21, 22** Knit. **23** *K1, ssk, k1; repeat from*—12 sts. **24** Knit. Cut yarn and pull through remaining sts. Do not pull tightly.

Arms *MAKE 2*
Cast on 12 sts evenly onto 3 dpn. Join and k every rnd until piece measures 2¼". **Next rnd** Ssk, k to end—11 sts. K 2 rnds. **Next rnd** Ssk, k to end—10 sts. K 11 rnds.
Shape thumb
Next rnd K7, [slip last 2 sts back to left-hand needle, k2] twice. Slip 2nd st on right-hand needle over first st and off needle. Cut yarn, leaving an 18" tail. Pull tail through st to finish off and run tail down to base of thumb. With same yarn, k 6 rnds on remaining 8 sts. Pull yarn through sts and pull together tightly.

Right Sleeve
Cast on 15 sts and divide evenly onto 3 dpn. Work 30 rnds of Right Sleeve Chart (page 38)—27 sts. Work back and forth in rows as follows: ***Begin Sleeve Point Chart: Row 1*** (RS) Work row 1 of Sleeve Point Chart (page 38) over 9 sts. Continue in pattern on these sts only through chart row 9. Cut yarn, leaving a 1½-yd tail. Pull

(continues on page 36)

33

My second tree-top angel has a longer, narrow skirt for a modern look—or a slender tree.

Contemporary Angel

Notes See Traditional Angel notes, page 32.

CONTEMPORARY ANGEL
Bodice

Cast on 15 sts. Work 41 rows of Bodice Chart—17 sts. Bind off all sts, working k2tog over first and last 2 sts before binding off.

Head

Cast on 12 sts and divide evenly onto 4 dpn. **Rnds 1, 3, 4** Knit. **2** *K1, lifted increase in next st, k1; repeat from*—16 sts. **5** *K1, lifted increase in next st; repeat from*—24 sts. **6, 7** Knit. **8** *K3, lifted increase in next st; repeat from*—30 sts. **9** Knit. **10** *K1, [lifted increase, k3, lifted increase, k2] twice; repeat from* once more—38 sts. **11–14** Knit. **15** *K1, [ssk, k3, ssk, k2] twice; repeat from* once more—30 sts. **16** Knit. **17** *K3, ssk; repeat from*—24 sts. **18, 19** Knit. **20** *K1, ssk; repeat from*—16 sts. **21, 22** Knit. **23** *K1, ssk, k1; repeat from*—12 sts. **24** Knit. Cut yarn and pull through remaining sts. Do not pull tightly.

Arms *MAKE 2*

Cast on 12 sts evenly onto 3 dpn. Join and k every rnd until piece measures 2¼". **Next rnd** Ssk, k to end—11 sts. K 2 rnds.

Next rnd Ssk, k to end—10 sts. K 11 rnds.
Shape thumb
Next rnd K7, [slip last 2 sts back to left-hand needle, k2] twice. Slip 2nd st on right-hand needle over first st and off needle. Cut yarn, leaving an 18" tail. Pull tail through st to finish off and run tail down to base of thumb. With same yarn, k 6 rnds on remaining 8 sts. Pull yarn through sts and pull together tightly.

Right Sleeve

Cast on 15 sts and divide evenly onto 3 dpn. Work 30 rnds of Right Sleeve Chart—27 sts. Work back and forth in rows as follows: ***Begin Sleeve Point Chart: Row 1** (RS) Work row 1 of Sleeve Point Chart over 9 sts. Continue in pattern on these sts only through chart row 9. Cut yarn, leaving a 1½-yd tail. Pull tail through st to finish off and run tail along left side of point down to base. Repeat from* twice more.

Left Sleeve

Work as for right sleeve, except use Left Sleeve Chart, instead of Right Sleeve Chart.

Skirt

Cast on 24 sts and divide evenly onto 3 dpn. **Rnd 1** Work 4-st repeat of Contemporary

SIZE
10" high

YARN
Coats & Clark Knit-Cro-Sheen 100% cotton • 225yds/205m 1 ball

NEEDLES
2.25mm/US1 double-pointed needles (dpn) Set of 5

EXTRAS
Cornstarch
Tapestry needle
Polyester fiberfill

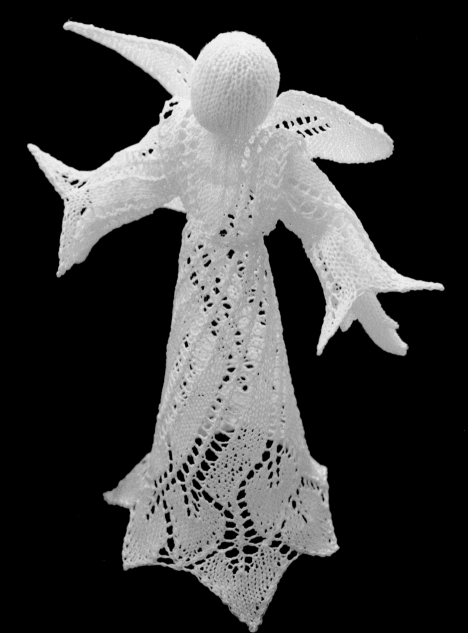

35

Angel Chart 6 times. Continue in chart pattern through rnd 41—54 sts. Then work rnds 36-59 of Traditional Angel Chart—78 sts. Shape skirt points as for Traditional Angel, except cut yarn leaving a 4½-yd tail after first point has been worked, and work a total of 6 points.

Left Wing

Cast on 8 sts. Work rows 1-7 of Contemporary Angel Left Wing Chart. ***Divide wing: Left half, Row 8*** (WS) P12, turn. Work through chart row 39 on these sts only. Cut yarn, leaving a 4 yd tail. Pull tail through st to finish off and run tail down along right edge to base to put yarn in position to work next half. ***Right half, Row 8*** P12. Work through chart row 39. Fasten off.

Right Wing

Work as for left wing, except use Contemporary Angel Right Wing Chart.

Finishing See Both Angels, page 37, for finishing.

TRADITIONAL ANGEL *(continued from page 32)*

tail through st to finish off and run tail along left side of point down to base. Repeat from* twice more.

Left Sleeve

Work as for right sleeve, except use Left Sleeve Chart, instead of Right Sleeve Chart.

Skirt

Cast on 24 sts and divide evenly onto 4 dpn. ***Rnd 1*** Work 6-st repeat of Traditional Angel Skirt Chart 4 times. Continue in chart pattern through rnd 59—104 sts.

Shape points

Work back and forth in rows as follows (turn work after every row and work following row as directed): ***Row 1*** (RS) K2, S2KP2, slip these 3 sts to last needle of rnd. ***2*** P6, SSSP. ***3*** Ssk, k3, k2tog. ***4*** P5. ***5*** Ssk, k1, k2tog. ***6*** P3. ***7*** S2KP2. Cut yarn, leaving a 6-yd tail. Pull tail through st to finish off and run tail down along left side of point to base. ****Next point: Row 1*** (RS) SK2P, k9, S2KP2. ***2*** P11. ***3*** Ssk, k to last 2 sts, k2tog. ***4*** Purl. Repeat rows 3-4 three times

more—3 sts. **Next row** (RS) S2KP2. Finish as for previous point.
Next point: Row 1 (RS) SK2P, k5, S2KP2. **2** P7. **3** Ssk, k3, k2tog. **4** P5.
5 Ssk, k1, k2tog. **6** P3. **7** S2KP2. Finish as for previous point. Repeat
from* until all sts have been worked—8 points completed.

Left Wing
Cast on 9 sts. Work rows 1–13 of Traditional Angel Left Wing
Chart. **Divide wing: Left section, Row 14** (WS) P14, p2tog, turn. Work
through chart row 39 on these sts only. Cut yarn, leaving a 4½-
yd tail. Pull yarn through st to finish off and run tail along right
edge to base to put yarn in position to work next section. **Center
section, Row 14** P13, turn. Work through chart row 25 on these sts
only. Complete as for left section. **Right section, Row 14** P2tog, p14.
Work through chart row 39 on these sts only. Fasten off last st.

Right Wing
Work as for left wing, except use Traditional Angel Right
Wing Chart.

Finishing
See Both Angels for finishing.

BOTH ANGELS
Work in ends at lower edge of skirt, tips of wings and ends of
sleeves before stiffening, and at ends of hands before stuffing.
Use other ends for joining pieces. See *How to Assemble an
Angel*, page 46.

in other words…

BODICE CHART *BEGIN ON 15 STS*
Row 1 and all WS rows K1, p to last st, k1. **2** K1, yo, k2, [k2tog, yo]
twice, k1, [yo, ssk] twice, k2, yo, k1—17 sts. **4** K1, yo, k2, [k2tog, yo]
twice, k3, [yo, ssk] twice, k2, yo, k1—19 sts. **6** K1, yo, k2, [k2tog, yo]
twice, k5, [yo, ssk] twice, k2, yo, k1—21 sts. **8** K1, yo, k2, [k2tog, yo]
twice, k7, [yo, ssk] twice, k2, yo, k1—23 sts. **10** K1, yo, k2, [k2tog, yo]
twice, k9, [yo, ssk] twice, k2, yo, k1—25 sts. **12, 14, 16, 18, 20** K1, yo,

k2, [k2tog, yo] twice, k3, k2tog, k1, ssk, k3, [yo,
ssk] twice, k2, yo, k1. **22, 24, 26, 28, 30, 32** K1, yo,
k2, [k2tog, yo] twice, k2tog, k7, ssk, [yo, ssk]
twice, k2, yo, k1. **34** K1, yo, k2, [k2tog, yo] twice,
k2tog, ssk, k3, k2tog, ssk, [yo, ssk] twice, k2, yo,
k1—23 sts. **36** K1, yo, k2, [k2tog, yo] twice, k2tog,
ssk, k1, k2tog, ssk, [yo, ssk] twice, k2, yo, k1—21
sts. **38** K1, yo, k2, [k2tog, yo] twice, k2tog, S2KP2,
ssk, [yo, ssk] twice, k2, yo, k1—19 sts. **40** K1, yo,
[k2tog] twice, [yo, k2tog] twice, k1, [ssk, yo]
twice, [ssk] twice, yo, k1—17 sts. **41** Rep row 1.

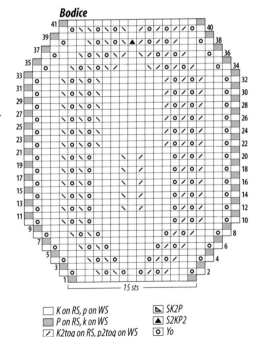

Bodice

15 sts

☐ K on RS, p on WS
▨ P on RS, k on WS
☑ K2tog on RS, p2tog on WS
◹ Ssk
◳ SK2P
▲ S2KP2
◉ Yo

37

Right Sleeve

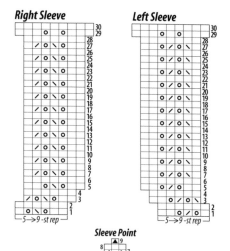

Left Sleeve

Sleeve Point

RIGHT SLEEVE CHART *5 TO 9-ST REPEAT*

Rnd 1 *K2, yo, ssk, yo, k1; rep from*—18 sts. **2 and all even-numbered rnds** Knit. **3** *K2, yo, ssk, yo, k2tog; rep from*. **5** *K2, yo, ssk, yo, k2; rep from*—21 sts. **7–27 (odd-numbered rnds)** *K2, yo, ssk, yo, k2tog, k1; rep from*. **29** *K3, yo, k1, yo, k3; rep from*—27 sts. **30** Knit.

LEFT SLEEVE CHART *5 TO 9-ST REPEAT*

Rnd 1 *K1, yo, k2tog, yo, k2; rep from*—18 sts. **2 and all even-numbered rnds** Knit. **3** *Ssk, yo, k2tog, yo, k2; rep from*. **5** *K2, yo, k2tog, yo, k2; rep from*—21 sts. **7–27 (off numbered rnds)** *K1, ssk, yo, k2tog, yo, k2; rep from*. **29** *K3, yo, k1, yo, k3; rep from*—27 sts. **30** Knit.

SLEEVE POINT CHART *BEGIN ON 9 STS*

Row 1 (RS) Ssk, k2, yo, k1, yo, k2, k2tog. **2 and all WS rows** Purl. **3** Ssk, k5, k2tog. **5** Ssk, k3, k2tog. **7** Ssk, k1, k2tog. **9** S2KP2.

TRADITIONAL SKIRT CHART *6 TO 26-ST REPEAT*

Rnd 1 all odd-numbered rnds Knit. **2** *Yo, ssk, yo, k1; rep from*—32 sts. **4** *Yo, ssk, yo, k2; rep from*—40 sts. **6** *Yo, ssk, yo, k3; rep from*—48 sts. **8** *Yo, ssk, yo, k4; rep from*—56 sts. **10, 12, 14** *Yo, ssk, yo, k2tog, k3; rep from*. **16** *Yo, ssk, yo, k5; rep from*—64 sts. **18, 20, 22, 24** *Yo, ssk, yo, k2tog, k4; rep from*. **26** *Yo, ssk, yo, k6; rep from*—72 sts. **28, 30, 32, 34** *Yo, ssk, yo, k5, k2tog; rep from*. **36** *Yo, ssk, yo, k5, k2tog, [yo, k1] 3 times, yo, ssk, k2, k2tog; rep from*—80 sts. **38** *Yo, ssk, yo, k5, k2tog, yo, k3, yo, k1, yo, k3, yo, ssk, k2tog; rep from*—88 sts. **40** *Yo, ssk, yo, k5, k2tog, yo, k5, yo, k1, yo, k5, yo, ssk; rep from*—100 sts. **42** *[Yo, k1] 3 times, yo, ssk, k2, S2KP2, yo, ssk, k9, k2tog, yo, ssk; rep from*. **44** *Yo, k3, yo, k1, yo, k3, yo, ssk, S2KP2, yo, ssk, k7, k2tog, yo, ssk; rep from*. **46** *Yo, k5, yo, k1, yo, k5, yo, SK2P, yo, ssk, k5, k2tog, yo, ssk; rep from*—104 sts. **48** *Yo, k1, yo, ssk, k9, k2tog, yo, SK2P, yo, ssk, k3, k2tog, [yo, k1] twice; rep from*. **50** *Yo, k3, yo, ssk, k7, k2tog, yo, SK2P, yo, ssk, k1, k2tog, yo, k3, yo, k1; rep from*. **52** *Yo, k5, yo, ssk, k5, k2tog, yo, SK2P, yo, S2KP2, yo, k5, yo, k1; rep from*. **54** *K5, k2tog, yo, ssk, k3, k2tog, [yo, k1] twice, yo, k2tog, yo, ssk, k6; rep from*. **56** *K4, k2tog, yo, S2KP2, k1, k2tog, yo, k3, yo, k1, yo, k3, yo, ssk, k5; rep from*. **58** *K3, [S2KP2, yo] twice, k5, yo, k1, yo, k5, yo, ssk, k4; rep from*. **59** Knit.

TRADITIONAL ANGEL LEFT WING CHART *BEGIN ON 9 STS*

Row 1 (RS) K2, [yo, k1] 4 times, [k1, yo] twice, k1—15 sts. *2 and all WS rows (except row 14)* Purl. *3* *K3, yo, k1, yo, k2*, yo, SK2P, yo, rep from * to * once—19 sts. *5* *K4, yo, k1, yo, k3*, yo, SK2P, yo, rep from * to * once—23 sts. *7* *K5, yo, k1, yo, k4*, yo, SK2P, yo, rep from * to * once—27 sts. *9* *K2, ssk, k2, yo, k1, yo, k5*, [yo, k1] 3 times, yo, rep from * to * once—33 sts. *11* *K2, ssk, k2, yo, k1, yo, k6*, yo, k3, yo, k1, yo, k3, yo, rep from * to * once—39 sts. *13* *K2, ssk, k2, yo, k1, yo, k7*, yo, k5, yo, k1, yo, k5, yo, rep from * to * once—45 sts. *Left section:* *Row 14* P14, p2tog. *15–33 (RS rows)* K2, ssk, k to end. *35* K2, k2tog, k1. *37* K1, k2tog, k1. *39* S2KP2. *Center section: Row 14* P13. *15, 17, 19, 21* K1, ssk, k to last 3 sts, k2tog, k1. *23* K1, S2KP2, k1. *25* S2KP2. *Right section: Row 14* P2tog, p14. *15–39* Work as for left section.

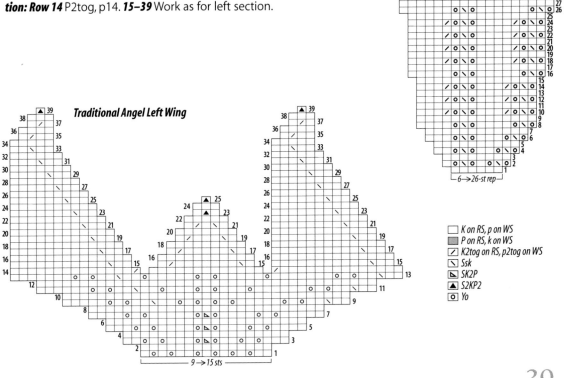

Traditional Angel Skirt

Traditional Angel Left Wing

9 → 15 sts

6 → 26-st rep

- ☐ K on RS, p on WS
- ■ P on RS, k on WS
- ⟋ K2tog on RS, p2tog on WS
- ⟍ Ssk
- ◣ SK2P
- ▲ S2KP2
- ⊙ Yo

Contemporary Angel Skirt

41
40
39
38
37
36
35
34
33
32
31
30
29
28
27
26
25
24
23
22
21
20
19
18
17
16
15
14
13
12
11
10
9
8
7
6
5
4
3
2
1

└─4→9-st rep─┘

TRADITIONAL ANGEL RIGHT WING CHART

BEGIN ON 9 STS

Row 1 (RS) [K1, yo] twice, k2, [yo, k1] 4 times, k1—15 sts. **2 and all WS rows (except row 14)** Purl. **3** *K2, yo, k1, yo, k3*, yo, SK2P, yo, rep from * to * once—19 sts. **5** *K3, yo, k1, yo, k4*, yo, SK2P, yo, rep from * to * once—23 sts. **7** *K4, yo, k1, yo, k5*, yo, SK2P, yo, rep from * to * once—27 sts. **9** *K5, yo, k1, yo, k2, k2tog, k2*, [yo, k1] 3 times, yo, rep from * to * once—33 sts. **11** *K6, yo, k1, yo, k2, k2tog, k2*, yo, k3, yo, k1, yo, k3, yo, rep from * to * once—39 sts. **13** *K7, yo, k1, yo, k2, k2tog, k2*, yo, k5, yo, k1, yo, k5, yo, rep from * to * once—45 sts. **Left section: Row 14** P14, p2tog. **15–33 (RS rows)** K to last 4 sts, k2tog, k2. **35** K1, ssk, k2. **37** K1, ssk, k1. **39** S2KP2. **Center section: Rows 14–25** Work as for Left Wing Chart. **Right section: Row 14** P2tog, p14. **15–39** Work as for left section.

CONTEMPORARY ANGEL SKIRT CHART

4 TO 9-ST REPEAT

Rnd 1 and all odd-numbered rnds Knit. **2** *Yo, ssk, yo, k2; rep from*—30 sts. **4, 6, 8, 10,12** *Yo, ssk, yo, k2tog, k1; rep from* . **14** *Yo, ssk, yo, k3; rep from*—36 sts. **16, 18, 20, 22** *Yo, ssk, yo, k2tog, k2; rep from*. **24** *Yo, ssk, yo, k4; rep from*—42 sts. **26, 28, 30** *Yo, ssk, yo, k2tog, k3; rep from*. **32** *Yo, ssk, yo, k5;*

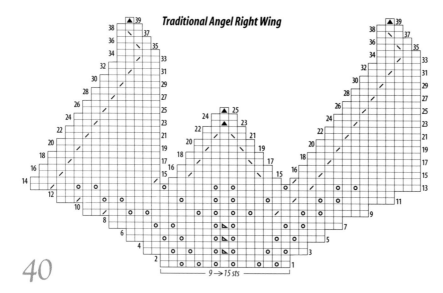

Traditional Angel Right Wing

9→15 sts

- ☐ K on RS, p on WS
- ▨ P on RS, k on WS
- ╱ K2tog on RS, p2tog on WS
- ╲ Ssk
- ◼ SK2P
- ▲ S2KP2
- ⊙ Yo

rep from*—48 sts. **34, 36** *Yo, ssk, yo, k2tog, k4; rep from*. **38** *Yo, ssk, yo, k6; rep from*—54 sts. **40** *Yo, ssk, yo, k2tog, k5; rep from*. **41** Knit.

CONTEMPORARY ANGEL LEFT WING CHART
BEGIN ON 8 STS
Row 1 (RS) K2, yo, k1, yo, k3, [yo, k1] twice—12 sts. **2 and all WS rows** Purl. **3** K3, yo, k1, yo, k5, yo, k1, yo, k2—16 sts. **5** K4, yo, k1, yo, k7, yo, k1, yo, k3—20 sts. **7** K5, yo, k1, yo, k9, yo, k1, yo, k4—24 sts. **Left half: Row 8** P12. **9** K2, ssk, k2, yo, k1, yo, k5—13 sts. **11** K2, ssk, k2, yo, k1, yo, k6—14 sts. **13** K2, ssk, k2, yo, k1, yo, k7—15 sts. **15–33 (RS rows)** K2, ssk, k to end. **35** K2, k2tog, k1. **37** K1, k2tog, k1. **39** S2KP2. **Right half: Rows 8–39** Work as for left half.

CONTEMPORARY ANGEL RIGHT WING CHART
BEGIN ON 8 STS
Row 1 (RS) [K1, yo] twice, k3, yo, k1, yo, k2—12 sts. **2 and all WS rows** Purl. **3** K2, yo, k1, yo, k5, yo, k1, yo, k3—16 sts. **5** K3, yo, k1, yo, k7, yo, k1, yo, k4—20 sts. **7** K4, yo, k1, yo, k9, yo, k1, yo, k5—24 sts. **Left half: Row 8** P12, turn. **9** K5, yo, k1, yo, k2, k2tog, k2—13 sts. **11** K6, yo, k1, yo, k2, k2tog, k2—14 sts. **13** K7, yo, k1, yo, k2, k2tog, k2—15 sts. **15–33 (RS rows)** K to last 4 sts, k2tog, k2. **35** K1, ssk, k2. **37** K1, ssk, k1. **39** S2KP2. **Right half: Rows 8–39** Work as for left half.

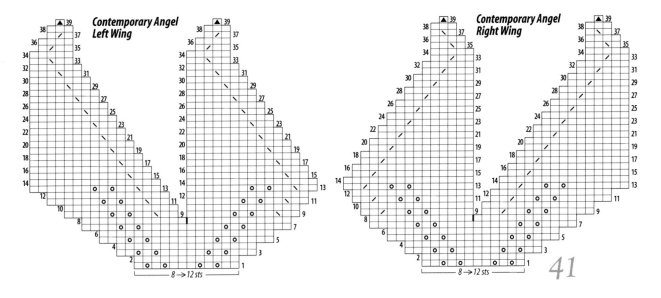

Contemporary Angel Left Wing

8 → 12 sts

Contemporary Angel Right Wing

8 → 12 sts

41

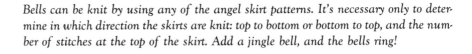

Bells can be knit by using any of the angel skirt patterns. It's necessary only to determine in which direction the skirts are knit: top to bottom or bottom to top, and the number of stitches at the top of the skirt. Add a jingle bell, and the bells ring!

Angel bells

SIZE
One size

YARN
Coats & Clark • Knit-Cro-Sheen
100% cotton
225 yds/205m
1 ball

NEEDLES
2.25mm/US1
double-pointed needles (dpn)
Set of 5

EXTRAS - ALL
Cornstarch • Tapestry needle

½" Jingle bell

BELL WITH KNOB
¼" Round, white bead

BELL WITH HANDLE
Cotton swab

BELL #1
Crochet hook of comparable size

Notes 1 See *School*, page 50 for ssk, M1, S2KP2, lifted increase, and single crochet bind-off. **2** Bells are worked circularly. **3** Bell 1 is worked from the top down, after working knob or handle; Bells 2 and 3 are worked from the bottom up, then the knob or handle is worked over remaining sts. **4** In Canada: Use Coats & Clark's "Mercerized" (1,000m ball). **5** Charts are on page 45.

BELL 1 *(from 2nd-wing-knitting angel skirt, p. 6)*
WORKED FROM THE TOP DOWN
Bell with Knob
*Cast on 6 sts evenly onto 3 dpn, leaving an 8" tail. Join and work as follows: **Rnd 1** Knit. **2** [K1, M1, k1] 3 times—9 sts. **3, 4, and 5** Knit.* **6** [Ssk] 4 times, k1—5 sts. **7** [Lifted increase in next st] 5 times—10 sts. **8** [Lifted increase in next st, k1] twice, [lifted increase in next st] 3 times, k1, lifted increase in next st, k1—16 sts. Rearrange sts evenly onto 4 dpn.

Bell with Handle
Work from* to* of Bell with Knob. **6** [Ssk, k1] 3 times—6 sts. K every rnd for 1". **Next rnd** [(Lifted increase in next st, yo) twice, k1, yo] twice—16 sts. **Next rnd** Knit.

Rearrange sts evenly onto 4 dpn.
Both Versions
Work rnds 2–21 of Bell #1 chart—48 sts. **Rnd 22** K1, *yo, k9, yo, twist left-hand needle with remaining 2 sts counterclockwise to become right-hand needle (equivalent of sl2tog), then k1 from next needle, p2sso; repeat from*. Pass last sl2tog over k1 from first needle—48 sts. **23, 25** Knit. **24** *Yo, ssk; repeat from*. With crochet hook, work single crochet bind-off.
Finishing
Bell with Knob
Insert bead into knob, with hole pointing up. Darn 8" tail through cast-on sts and pull together tightly to close. Run tail down through center of bead and out at base of knob. Wrap tail several times around base to secure bead. Run tail down to inside and use for attaching jingle bell after lace bell has been stiffened.
Bell with Handle
Cut cotton swab to length of handle and insert it into bell handle. Darn 8" tail through cast-on sts and pull together tightly. Run tail down through center of handle to inside of bell and use for attaching jingle bell after lace bell has been stiffened.

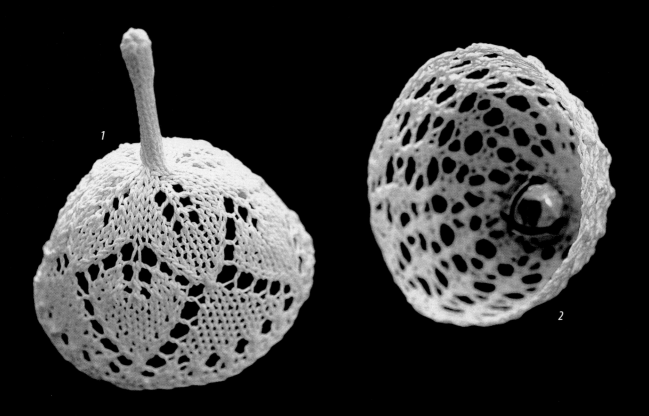
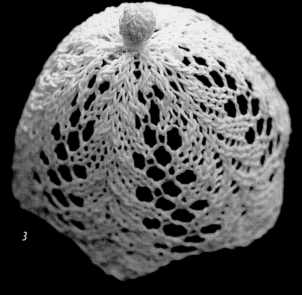

43

Both Versions

See All Bells for remaining finishing.

BELL 2 *(from Embroidering Angel skirt, p. 30)*
WORKED FROM THE BOTTOM UP

Cast on 54 sts evenly onto 3 dpn. **Rnd 1** Work 6-st repeat of Bell 2 Chart 9 times. Continue in chart pattern through rnd 24—18 sts. **Dec rnd** [S2KP2] 6 times—6 sts.

Bell with Knob

Rnd 1 [K1, M1, k1] 3 times—9 sts. **2, 3, 4** Knit. **5** [Ssk, k1] 3 times—6 sts. Cut end, leaving 8" tail, and run tail through open sts. Insert bead into knob with hole pointing up and pull sts together tightly. Run tail down through center of bead and out at base of knob. Wrap tail several times around base to secure bead. Run tail to inside and use for attaching jingle bell after lace bell has been stiffened.

Bell with Handle

K every rnd for 1". **Next rnd** [K1, M1, k1] 3 times—9 sts. K 3 rnds. **Next rnd** [Ssk, k1] 3 times—6 sts. Cut end, leaving 8" tail, and run through open sts. Do not pull up. Cut end off cotton swab so that stem is the length of bell's handle. Insert swab into handle and pull sts together tightly. Run

tail down through handle to inside and use for attaching jingle bell after lace bell has been stiffened.

Both Versions

See All Bells for finishing.

BELL 3 *(from Quilting Angel skirt, p. 31)*
WORKED FROM THE BOTTOM UP

Cast on 54 sts evenly onto 3 dpn. **Rnd 1** Work 9-st repeat of Bell 3 Chart 6 times. Continue in chart pattern through rnd 22—42 sts. **Rnd 23** K2tog, *ssk, k2tog, SK2P; repeat from* to last 5 sts, ssk, k2tog, slip 1, pass slip st over k2tog on first dpn—18 sts. **Rnd 24** Knit. **Dec rnd** [S2KP2] 6 times—6 sts.

Bell with Knob

Work as for Bell 2.

Bell with Handle

Work as for Bell 2.

Both Versions

See All Bells for finishing.

ALL BELLS

Darn in ends at lower edge of skirt before stiffening.

Select and prepare molds

Use a styrofoam egg taped to cardboard

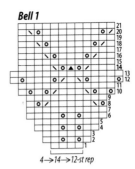

Bell 1

4→14→12-st rep

□ K on RS, p on WS   ○ Yo   ◣ SK2P   ⊼ Ssk on RS, ssp on WS
⚎ K1 through back loop (tbl)   ▲ S2KP2   ◪ K3tog   ⟋ K2tog on RS, p2tog on WS

cylinder or a styrofoam bell. Cover mold with plastic wrap.

Stiffener

Mix 1 Tbsp. cornstarch with 1 Tbsp. cold water. Add BOILING water until mixture measures ½ cup. Cook in microwave (or on stove) until thick and translucent. Stir well at each stage. Place bells into stiffener mixture. Moisten well, then squeeze out excess. Place bell over mold, stretching hem to an even length. Let pieces dry completely. Attach jingle bell.

in other words…

BELL 1 CHART

4 TO 14 TO 12-ST REPEAT

Rnd 1 and all odd-numbered rnds Knit. **2** *[K1, yo] twice, k2; rep from*—24 sts. **4** *K2, yo, k1, yo, k3; rep from*—32 sts. **6** *K3, yo, k1, yo, k4; rep from*—40 sts. **8** *Yo, ssk, k5, k2tog, yo, k1; rep from*. **10** *Yo, k1, yo, ssk, k3, k2tog, yo, k1, yo, k1; rep from*—48 sts. **12** *Yo, k3, yo, ssk, k1, k2tog, yo, k3, yo, k1; rep from*—56 sts. **14** *K3, k2tog, yo, S2KP2, yo, ssk, k4; rep

from*—48 sts. **16** *K2, k2tog, yo, k3, yo, ssk, k3; rep from*. **18** *K1, k2tog, yo, k5, yo, ssk, k2; rep from*. **20** *K2tog, yo, k7, yo, ssk, k1; rep from*. **21** Knit.

BELL 2 CHART

6 TO 4 TO 2-ST REPEAT

Rnd 1 and all odd-numbered rnds Knit. **2** *Yo, k1 tbl, yo, ssk, k1, k2tog; rep from*. **4** *Yo, SK2P; rep from*—36 sts. **6** *K3, yo, k1 tbl, yo; rep from*—54 sts. **8** *SK2P, yo; rep from*—36 sts. **10** *Yo, k1 tbl, yo, k3; rep from*—54 sts. **12–18** Rep rows 4–10. **20** Rep rnd 4—36 sts. **22** *SK2P, yo, k1 tbl, yo; rep from*. **24** *K1, SK2P; rep from*—18 sts.

BELL 3 CHART

9 TO 7-ST REPEAT

Rnd 1 *K1, yo, k2, ssk, k2tog, k2, yo; rep from*. **2 and all even-numbered rnds** Knit. **3** *Yo, k2, ssk, k2tog, k2, yo, k1; rep from*. **5–20** Rep rnds 1–4 four times. **21** *K1, yo, [ssk] twice, [k2tog] twice, yo; rep from*—42 sts. **22** Knit.

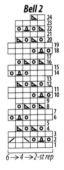

Bell 2

6→4→2-st rep

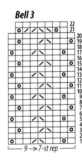

Bell 3

9→7-st rep

45

How to Assemble an Angel

Select and prepare molds
Small angels
For skirt, use a styrofoam egg taped to a cardboard cylinder or a styrofoam bell. For bodice shoulders, use a pencil or wooden chopstick. Cover molds with plastic wrap.

Large angels
For wide skirt, use a small decanter with a cylinder taped to the lower section. For narrow skirt, use a styrofoam cone with a 4½" aluminum tart pan taped to it to form the trumpet flare. For sleeves, use a ¾" cylinder (candle stubs or glue sticks). For bodice, use stiff plastic, bent to form a teardrop, using the wide part for the shoulders. Cover molds with plastic wrap.

Shape and stiffen
Stiffener mixture for all
Mix 1 tablespoon cornstarch with 1 table-spoon cold water. Add BOILING water until mixture measures ½ cup. Cook in microwave (or on stove) until very thick and translucent. Stir well at each stage.

Small angels
Do not starch head. Place skirt, arms, bodice and complete wings into hot stiffener mixture. Moisten well, then squeeze out excess. Place skirt over mold, stretching hem to an even length. Stretch out wings and dry flat (1). Fold arms in half lengthwise, then bend at 'elbows.' Fold bodice in half and drape over mold. Let pieces dry completely.

Large angels
Do not starch head and arms. Place skirt, bodice, sleeves and wings into hot stiffener mixture. Moisten well, then squeeze out excess. Place skirt over mold, stretching longest points to the same length. It may be necessary to hold the points flat with a strip of fabric wrapped around the outside. Stretch out wings and dry flat on plastic wrap. Place sleeves over molds, twisting to accentuate the knitted spiral. Pull the points outward. Fold bodice in half and drape over mold. Let pieces dry completely.

Put it together
Small angels
Stuff head with small amount of poly-ester fiberfill or cotton ball. Pull yarn end tight, darn around loops again, then bring end down to cast-on edge. Using

both yarn ends, sew head to folded edge of bodice (2). Tie ends together at wrong side of bodice. Do not cut. Sew wing(s) to bodice back (3). Tie cast-on edge of arms together (4), then tie to ends from head (5; this positions arms high and prevents them from moving). Trim ends. Sew lower edge of bodice to top of skirt (6). Tie ends at wrong side of skirt and trim.

Large angels

Stuff head firmly. Pull yarn end tight, run through sts again, then bring end down to cast-on edge. Stuff arms lightly. Sew ends from head to top of bodice. Cut ends. Sew wings, with tips flaring upward, along decreases on back of bodice. Pull arms into sleeves (thumbs up) and sew to top of sleeve. Place sleeves into shoulder of bodice, sewing along 2nd row of bodice holes so that a flange is formed at the shoulder. Angle the arms as desired and secure at chest level on both front and back. Bend arms at elbow and secure with invisible thread if desired. Sew skirt to bodice.

Putting together a small angel.

For a large angel, just add sleeves.

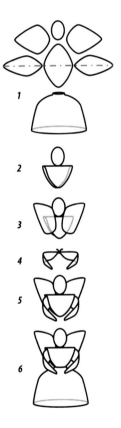

1
2
3
4
5
6

47

Lace Basics

Yarn overs (yo)

In lace knitting, the holes are formed by yarn overs. The yarn travels over the right-hand needle in the same direction it does when you knit or purl. This makes a "stitch" between two stitches. The way the yarn over is made depends on what kind of stitch comes before and after it.

K, yo, k: After knitting a stitch, the yarn is behind the right-hand needle. Bring the yarn under the needle to the front, take it over the needle to the back (where it is in position to knit), and knit the next stitch.

K, yo, p: Knit; bring yarn under the needle to the front, over the needle to the back, then back under the needle to the front—all before you purl the next stitch.

P, yo, k: Purl; the yarn is already to the front of the needle so simply bring it over the needle to the back; it is in position to knit the next stitch.

Often the stitch before or after a yarn over is not a knit or a purl, but a decrease. If it is a knit decrease (k2tog, SSK, etc.), treat it as a knit; if it is a purl decrease (p2tog, SSP, etc.), treat it as a purl. On the next row, work into the yarn over as if it is a regular stitch.

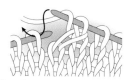

Right-leaning decrease: K2tog, yo ⊡⊡

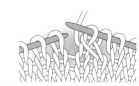

Left-leaning decrease: Yo, ssk ⊡⊡

GENERAL TIPS

Check as you go. If you run into a problem working a row, check for a missing yarn over in the preceding row or two. This is usually the problem.

All the Angel patterns have you work a plain knit/purl row or round between each yarn-over row or round. When you are working this plain row or round, count the stitches to make sure that a yarn over isn't missing. If you find that one is, just work to where it should be. Then put your left needle under the thread that should have been the yarn over (between 2 stitches), tug a bit, and you have a yarn over that can be worked into as usual.

Fine cotton. If you haven't worked with cotton before, you will find it takes a little more attention. Knitters often say, "Cotton isn't as forgiving as wool." We're not talking sins, here, just even tension.

What helps? Practice (you might even knit a couple of wings—or an entire angel—with a heavier cotton yarn and larger needles), extra tension on the yarn (many knitters wrap cotton thread around their finger an extra time or two), and attention (learn a new skill when you are attentive and well-rested). If you are new to both fine cotton and lace, you might practice lace with heavier yarn. Then try fine cotton and swatch in stockinette or garter stitch before you try the lace. Breaking a new skill into small steps reduces stress.

Charts can help. If you're a beginning lace knitter or have had problems with lace, give charts a try.

Each square of the chart is one stitch (or one knitting operation, such as a k2tog). Each row of the chart shows a completed row or round of knitting.

The chart depicts the right side of the fabric, so check the key to see how to work a certain symbol on the right side and on the wrong side.

Work the chart as you knit: from bottom to top. Read right-side rows from right to left, wrong-side rows from left to right. (In circular knitting, all rows are right-side rows; the chart is always read from right to left.)

Begin with row 1. If the number is on the right edge of the chart, row 1 is a right-side row; if on the left edge, it is a wrong-side row.

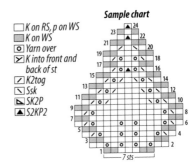

Sample chart

☐ K on RS, p on WS
▨ K on WS
☉ Yarn over
⊠ K into front and back of st
☑ K2tog
◺ Ssk
◣ SK2P
▲ S2KP2

School for Angels

ABBREVIATIONS

dpn	double-pointed needle(s)
k	knit
m	meter(s)
mm	millimeter(s)
p	purl
rep	repeat(s)
rnd	round
RS	right side
sl	slip
st(s)	stitch(es)
tbl	through back loop
Tbsp	tablespoon
tog	together
WS	wrong side
yd	yard
yo	yarn over
"	inch(es)

SSK
Uses A left-slanting single decrease.

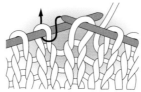

1 Slip 2 sts separately to right needle as if to knit.

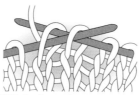

2 Knit these 2 sts together by slipping left needle into them from left to right; 2 sts become one.

SK2P, SL1-K2TOG-PSSO
Uses A left-slanting double decrease.
1 Slip 1 st knitwise.
2 Knit next 2 sts together.
3 Pass the slipped st over the k2tog.

S2KP2, SL2-K1-P2SSO
Uses A centered double decrease.

1 Slip 2 sts together to right needle as if to knit.

2 Knit next st.

3 Pass 2 slipped sts over knit st and off right needle.

4 Completed: 3 sts become 1; the center st is on top.

MAKE 1 (M1)
Uses A single increase.

With left needle from back of work, pick up strand between last st knitted and next st. Knit, twisting the strand by working into the loop at the front of the needle.

LIFTED INCREASE

Knit into right loop of st in row below (1), then knit st on needle (2).

SSP

Uses A left-slanting single decrease.

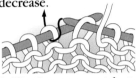

1 Slip 2 sts separately to right needle as if to knit.

2 Slip these 2 sts back onto left needle. Insert right needle through their 'back loops,' into the second st and then the first.

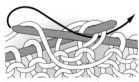

3 Purl them together.

SSSP

Uses A left-slanting double decrease. Work same as SSP except:
1 Slip 3 sts . . .
2 Slip these 3 sts back onto left needle. Insert right needle through their 'back loops,' into the third st, then the second st and then the first.
3 Purl them together.

SINGLE-CROCHET BIND-OFF

Insert hook knitwise into first knit st. Yarn round hook, pull up a loop and drop knit st. *Insert hook in next st, yarn round hook, pull up a loop and drop knit st—2 loops on hook. Yarn round hook and pull up a loop through both sts on hook—1 single-crochet bind-off complete. Repeat from*. Cut yarn.
For a continuous, smooth edge, go through first bound-off st, then down through the last bound-off st again. Weave in end.

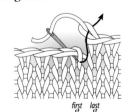

first *last*
st *st*

WORKING WITH DOUBLE-POINT-ED NEEDLES (DPN)

Cast stitches onto one dpn.
1 Rearrange stitches on three dpn.
2 Begin working in rounds as follows:
Check carefully that stitches do not twist around a dpn or between dpn. With 4th dpn, work all stitches from first dpn. Use that empty dpn to work the stitches from the 2nd dpn. Use that empty dpn to work the stitches from the 3rd dpn —one round completed. Notice that you work with only two dpn at a time. As you work the first few rounds, be careful that the stitches do not twist between the nee-dles. If instructions rec-ommend working with a set of five dpn, arrange the stitches on four and knit with the fifth.

1

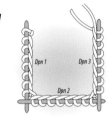

2

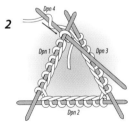

Hang Tags
for Angels and Bells

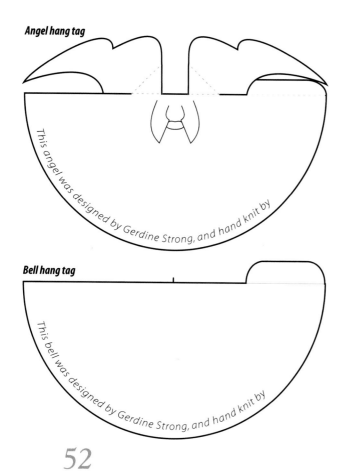

Angel hang tag

This angel was designed by Gerdine Strong, and hand knit by

Bell hang tag

This bell was designed by Gerdine Strong, and hand knit by

For angel tag: Fill in your name as the knitter, and photocopy the hang tags. Cut hang tags on the solid lines: around the wings, skirt and the skirt tab. The wings are cut up to the dotted line.

Make the head from 2 circles cut with a hole punch. Cut a 10" length of white sewing thread. Fold in half and glue the circles ¾" from the cut ends. (Keep the threads separated.) Fasten the threads to the neck area with cellulose tape.

Fold the wings on the vertical line toward each other and glue in the small triangular area. Fold the wings on the horizontal dotted line toward the skirt. This will raise the wings when the skirt tab is glued to the skirt. Align the center back and the lower edge.

Thread the looped end into a darning needle and pull tag into skirt and up through the head. This loop can be used for hanging the angel or bell. Make an overhand knot near the loop so that the tag will not pull out too easily. The angels will sit over the tags with the threads inside.

For bell tag: Attach thread loop and glue skirt tab in place.

52